WHO SPEAKS FOR GOD?

WHO SPEAKS
FOR GOD?

Confronting the World with Real Christianity

Charles Colson

HODDER AND STOUGHTON
LONDON AUCKLAND SYDNEY TORONTO

British Library Cataloguing in Publication Data

Colson, Charles
    Who speaks for God?——(Hodder Christian
    paperbacks)
    1. Christian life
    I. Title
    248.4   BV4501.2

ISBN 0 340 39091 3

Contents

Foreword

"...I was to speak following the President. That made me a little nervous. Last time I followed a President I got one-to-three years..." A typical Colson line, uttered with total good humor. Everybody howled, then hushed themselves, thus illustrating the old truth that those who laugh with the speaker listen to him too. I know, for I was there. We hung on every word.

Colson is a remarkable person, however you assess him. As fixer and hatchet-man for the head of state he was gruesomely brilliant, as all the world knows. As a converted Christian, founder and leader of Prison Fellowship, he is brilliant still — and "gruesomely" no longer applies. What God has done during the past decade through Colson's speeches, books, personal drive, and passion to change bad things for the better, seems in retrospect miraculous. Paul described gifted Christians as God's gifts to men: Christ's servant Charles Colson is certainly a case in point.

And there is more to him than brilliance, even sanctified brilliance. He has the vision and burden of a prophet. He has come to perceive what a Puritan once called the evil of evil, and the sinfulness of sin. He has seen through the bewitching illusions and idolatries of the power game, and recognized the inhumanity of the justice, so-called, that does not have love at its heart. Standing apart from secular and religious establishments, he lets God's Word loose to judge both. He seeks to confront secular America with Christian truth, to expose the bankruptcy and hollowness of life without Christ, and to challenge the church to biblical fidelity and obedience, as the following pages show. Noting some of the nightmares into which the American dream is fast turning, he diagnoses our spiritual malaise in clear and stark terms. Thank God for his clarity of vision! It is a privilege to contribute this word of grateful appreciation to Chuck Colson's latest book.

J. I. Packer

Introduction

A few years ago, during a visit to Australia, I was interviewed by a well-known radio show host. As the program drew to a close, he posed one last question. "Mr. Colson, you are an unusual person. You have conquered the pinnacles of secular success. The goals most people strive their whole lives for, you have achieved — only to see it all collapse as you fell from the White House to prison. But now you're out, leading a new life as a Christian. It's like having lived two lives. How would you sum up the meaning of those two lives?"

I glanced at the clock, realizing with a sinking feeling that only 20 seconds remained in the live broadcast. Then in a flash the answer came. "If my life stands for anything," I said quickly, "it is the truth of the teaching of Jesus Christ, '...whoever wants to save his life will lose it, but whoever loses his life for me will find it. What good will it be for a man if he gains the whole world, yet forfeits his soul?'" (Matt. 16:25-26 NIV)

With that we went off the air, my questioner looking totally bewildered. And certainly those words do embody a staggering paradox. But in my life I've experienced the literal truth of those words. Jesus' shocking words to His disciples.

I had spent my first 40 years seeking the whole world, to the neglect of my soul. But what I couldn't find in my quest for power and success — that is, true security and meaning — I discovered in prison where all worldly props had been stripped away. And by God's grace, I lost my life in order that I might find true life in Christ.

Since then I have often reflected on the two lives the radio interviewer spoke of; in the light of God's Word I've seen with growing clarity the stark emptiness of the world without Christ. So I have felt an increasing burden to challenge its false and bankrupt values, to help keep others from the futile search that so consumed my early years.

Why is it that so many strive for this mirage? At root, of course, is the sinful rebellion that so infects our race, a willful blindness to the glory of God. But there is another reason, one which places blame squarely on those of us who profess to be Christians. For far too often we have failed to clearly discern truth ourselves, let alone impart it to others: we have failed to expose the false values of our culture to the penetrating light of biblical revelation. As theologian Donald Bloesch has insightfully pointed out, "Before the church can make an impact on the culture, it must break with the idolatries and misconceptions that dominate the culture." And, he warns, in the U.S. today, "where secularism so often dons the guise of religiosity, the primary danger is not persecution by the culture but seduction."

Thus we have embraced the world rather than exposed its folly. We have failed to show clearly that each individual is on one side or the other of a "war of the worlds" far greater than H.G. Wells could have imagined.

It's the same war between darkness and light that has raged from the beginning. Today we may have much of "religion," whether it be the generic American civil religion, or one of the "name brands"; we may have majorities who claim to be "born again," and countless retreats, rallies and rituals; but if we fail to stand for Christ at that place where the world is denying His Lordship, we are missing the mark.

Martin Luther stated well this powerful challenge, the same in his day as in our own:

> If I profess with the loudest voice and clearest exposition every portion of the truth of God except precisely that little point which the world and the devil are attacking at that moment, I am not confessing Christ, however boldly I may be professing Christ. Where the battle rages, there the loyalty of the soldier is proved, and to be steady on all battlefields besides, is mere flight and disgrace if he flinches at that point.

The battle today is raging all around, but many are perishing because we Christians have failed to engage the enemy at the point of attack. We not only flinch; for the most part we are not even looking in the right direction.

It is no accident that the West is called Christendom — historically, biblical truth has been at the foundation of our culture, though there has been a relentless invasion of secular values into the mainstream of our cultural life. This has become increasingly true in the media age: The world, as it is presented to us through the media, is portrayed in a way which systematically excludes the Christian world view. As a result, it is not surprising that our culture is crumbling — and that many have announced (some with undisguised delight) the end of Christendom.

Introduction

This is not, as some have hysterically charged, because of a vast "humanist" conspiracy. On the contrary, most secularists are no more self-conscious about their beliefs than anyone else. But unconsciously these beliefs are reflected in all they say and do: their world view, one which implicitly excludes any absolute truth or centrality of the living God, defines the possibilities of truth and falsehood, good and bad, by such relative criteria that truth itself becomes a meaningless term.

And, since such "secularized" people dominate most fields of endeavor, it ought not to surprise us that their views prevail, and that Christian truth is excluded, in the marketplace of ideas.

Thus, when in 1979 I began a monthly column for *Jubilee*, the newsletter of Prison Fellowship, I sought to critically examine the issues of our day through the new eyes God had given me. I had spent 40 years looking at the world from a secular point of view; now in my "second life" I could try to provide "Another Point of View," the title under which these essays first appeared.

Here are collected a selection of those columns; they represent my struggles to confess Christ "where the battle rages." And they embody a response to the challenge that has faced Christians throughout the ages: to stand for Christ *contra mundum* — "against the world" — the great rallying cry of the fourth-century champion of the faith, Athanasius. Indeed, those in the great cloud of witnesses who have gone before us, each in their own time, place and particular way, have had to stand against the world's denial of Christ's Lordship. We who assert Him as Lord today can do no less.

Finally, these essays, written over a period of years, represent my own spiritual pilgrimage, a journey in which I have attempted to discern the issues of our day by the light of biblical revelation. Thus the title of this collection, *Who Speaks For God?*, reflects my unyielding commitment to the proposition that neither I, nor anyone else, speaks for God except insofar as they speak founded upon His inerrant word.

In some things included here, I am sure I have been mistaken. Obviously if I knew in what, they would have fallen before my editor's pen. But concerning the pattern of response, I am, under Christ, quite confident. As John Wesley said:

> Making an open stand against all the ungodliness and unrighteousness which overspreads our land as a flood is one of the noblest ways of confessing Christ in the face of His enemies.

May God grant that these attempts of mine to make that good confession inspire many others to do the same. To Jesus Christ be the glory.

Charles W. Colson
June 15, 1985
P.O. Box 17500
Washington, D.C. 20041

With Gratitude

I'm grateful to my editorial associate, Ellen Santilli Vaughn, for her consistent and invaluable assistance over the years in preparation of these essays. Ellen has drafted, edited, probed, and often provided the creative spark for the genesis of these columns. And I appreciate as well the excellent work of my research associate, David Coffin, in assisting in the editing of this compilation.

Colson Gets 1- to 3-Year Term

God often uses what we least expect for His divine purposes. That has certainly proved to be true for me. Out of the depths of my prison experience came the vision for Prison Fellowship's ministry, which now involves thousands of volunteers and brings the hope of Christ to prisoners throughout the U.S. and abroad.

As I sorted through some forty cartons of papers, I came across writings from my first days at Maxwell Federal Prison after my ten-week stint at Fort Holabird prison in Baltimore. Because these formerly unpublished letters and journal entries give such a candid glimpse of what life in prison is really like, I thought it would be appropriate to share them with my readers. In the context of all that has happened in the past ten years, I believe these writings from prison bear witness to God's sovereignty, even in times of emptiness and pain.

Journal entries, undated; first impressions of Maxwell Federal Prison.

...I had a good collection of Christian books that I had stuffed into my bag. They [prison officials] examined each paper, each book, and each personal item, one by one...

My wallet would be packed in the suitcase and returned home. I protested momentarily on the grounds that I might be called back to Washington anytime to testify and I would certainly need my identification with me. Officer B____ explained that if I were taken back to Washington I would be in the custody of marshals with a set of government orders, a government-provided ticket and that I would need no identification.

The wallet, curiously enough, was one of the most difficult things to part with. It sounds like a small point, but psychologically it's a major one. One has no way of proving to anyone who he is, and if he should suddenly be granted his freedom, he would be totally dependent on someone else, some impersonal set of orders, or some marshal. I was faced with the disquieting feeling that I was to become no more than an anonymous number. Simply another face among a whole mass of faces.

...As the final act I was handed a set of dark brown, very well-worn surplus Air Force work clothes. The shirt was too tight and the pants too baggy. But at this point it made little difference. I was now a full-fledged federal prisoner. A member of what is euphemistically called "the population."

...Within a few moments I was ushered into the control room, the nerve center of the prison camp. It is a large square room with thick plate glass windows on three sides, overlooking the central courtyard. I was at once struck by the eerie feeling that everyone in the camp was being watched at all times.

...Looking out from the control room at the drab brown bodies moving about slowly, most of them hunched over, was the first real depressing awareness I had of the emptiness — the empty souls, the barrenness of the inside of a prison.

Excerpts from letter of September 18, 1974, to my fellowship prayer group in Washington, written my first day at Maxwell after nearly three months at Fort Holabird in Baltimore.

Dear Brothers,

...I am badly qualified after twenty-four hours to speak with much authority on life in the Maxwell Prison Camp. But I didn't want a day to pass without writing to let you know I am glad I came here. It is an experience I think will be important to use, however long it must last.

This is *no* country club, nor is it like boot camp, as some have suggested. It is a prison and the conditions are really worse than I expected (I will not tell Patty that; her burdens are enough already). The "barracks" aren't the way you guys remember from your military days — there is everything here from lifelong, hardened criminals to young drug offenders.

The reason I am glad to be here, however, is the sudden realization of how many needs there are here — spiritual needs and the need for people to establish their own identity and dignity as human beings. My heart has ached for so many while I am here; more important, when I leave I hope I can do something about the concept of rehabilitation and punishment. All its high sounding names — deterrence, rehabilitation — are untrue. If it is punishment, so be it; but maybe it is more humane to whip a man's body than destroy his soul slowly.

...It helps me to write you now before I get calloused to it. I want you brothers to read this letter back to me when I am out of here and have forgotten what the initial shock was like — and in the event I ever forget I have an obligation to try to improve the fate and circumstances of man in this plight.

...8:45 P.M.: I have been asked by six inmates and one guard if I'd share my witness with them. It is encouraging; I am convinced the Lord has planned this for me and will use me for

His purpose. I first had to learn who I was in relation to God; now I'm learning who I am in relation to others, and how the Lord works through us to reach others in need.

...I'll write as often as I can. Patty will be here this weekend and can tell you all the visiting arrangements. Give my love to all the brothers—I miss you all, but I want you to know I am fine.

In His love, Chuck

Excerpts from letter of October 23, 1974, also to the prayer group.

Dear Brothers,

Forgive me for being so slow in responding to your wonderful birthday messages. You helped mightily in supporting me last week. Special days like birthdays do add to the anxieties of being confined.

...I decided when I came here that I would offer no help to people as a lawyer. The demand is great and I was asked by many for assistance. In the last few weeks I've been helping some if I believed there was an opportunity to talk to them about Christ.

I have really had some magnificent experiences, particularly with some who cannot read or write and desperately need help — legally and spiritually. You can't imagine how much it opens a man's heart just to help in something as simple as writing a letter to his judge. I found that the man in the next bunk had tried for two weeks to compose a letter to his probation officer. He worked on it every night; I finally asked him what he was doing. When he told me, I helped him, and in a half hour it was done. Now he is borrowing my Bible.

Three other Christians and I have been meeting each night at 9:30 for a half-hour of fellowship and prayer.

We have a larger fellowship group on Monday evenings, fifteen or twenty men, and we're using that for a Bible study as well. It really is exciting when I think back; five weeks ago people were ridiculed for carrying a Bible. There was nothing like a fellowship. The Christians didn't even know one another. But none of this is a result of planning or conscious organizing. The Lord has worked through me and others, and this is happening because of Him, not us.

Apart from the separation from Patty, who is waiting faithfully for the gates to open each visiting day, my only real sorrow is being away from all of you. I miss you, but I am comforted in the assurance that all of this is by His plan; Christ's bonds are so great that our love cannot be affected by the distance which separates us. You are all in my prayers.

In His love, Chuck

August 1984

Chapter One

Who Speaks for God?

A New York bishop, speaking to a gay rights demonstration a few months ago, announced unequivocally that "AIDS is not God's judgment on the homosexual community." The idea that God might punish for such "so-called sins," he explained to his appreciative audience — and the grinding national television cameras — comes from "primitive, barbaric passages of the Old Testament."

The next day produced a predictable response from conservative church leaders. Indeed God has spoken, they thundered with righteous fervor; AIDS *is* His judgment on homosexuals.

My point here is not to address the question whether AIDS is a judgment of God. Frankly, I don't know. Indeed, homosexuality is a clear biblical sin. But all sin is an offense against God; to me, the miracle is that He has not already brought judgment on us *all* for the apostasy of our times.

But the debate raises a timely question. Who *does* speak for God?

It's timely because we live in an age when Christians glibly toss around clichés like "God told me" this or that. Some preachers, especially a few I've seen on television, sound like they've just hung up from a private phone session with Him immediately before going on the air.

Our biblical forebears had no such casual view of God's holy voice. When the children of Israel received the Ten Commandments, they fell on their faces. "We have heard His voice from the midst of the fire," they said. "We have seen today that God speaks with man, yet he lives."

It is no frivolous matter to hear the voice of God; and certainly it is an awesome trust to deign to speak for Him. Luther said that preaching made his knees knock. Spurgeon, the brilliant British preacher, said he "trembled" lest he should misinterpret the Word.

So, the only way we can ever speak with confidence is to speak from the Word. Jesus gives us the best example: He knew the Scriptures, drew His authority from them, and based His words upon them. Those who follow Him must do the same.

That's where the bishop fell off-track. In his compassion for homosexuals, he wrote off the Old Testment as "barbaric and primitive." As Oswald Chambers wrote, "It is possible to have such sympathy with our fellow man as to be guilty of red-handed rebellion against God." As a result of his empathy, the bishop not only condoned the sin, but did so in the name of a holy and righteous God. No wonder the world is turned off by "religion."

Ironically, while the bishop and his conservative challengers were pontificating over who was responsible for AIDS, I discovered that a young woman on my staff named Christy was using her evenings and weekends to do something about it.

At a time when most Americans were panic-stricken over the contagious disease or snickering at snide AIDS jokes, Christy and her prayer group were visiting terminally ill AIDS patients at a Washington area hospital.

None of the men had families in the area, and certainly no visitors. So Christy's group brought them postage stamps, stationery, books, tapes and cookies. In a prayer memo, Christy explained why she visited AIDS victims: "They are socially unacceptable because of their lifestyle and medically unacceptable because of their diseases. They are scared. They are dying. They are unsaved."

Christy's report continued, "We have been able to pray with eight of the patients. Two men who died in the last ten days received Christ. We've had in-depth conversations with one man about Jesus, the Good News, sin, justification and repentance.

"One Haitian woman was four-and-a-half months pregnant. Because of a language barrier she was unable to communicate, so we just wept together and prayed for her baby about to be aborted. (The hospital mandates abortion for AIDS-stricken mothers.)"

Was she afraid? "No," Christy responded. "We believe we are doing the will of God."

And of that Christy can be sure. For while the Word doesn't tell us whether AIDS is a judgment of God, it does demand that we care for the sick and have compassion for the suffering. The AIDS sufferers who are waiting to die alone, feared and ostracized, of all people need to hear the good news of the Gospel.

Christy and her friends remind us of a great truth: The quiet, often unnoticed actions of "ordinary" Christians who believe *and* obey speak far more loudly than all the bombast of so-called religious leaders.

Who speaks for God? He does quite nicely for Himself. Through His holy and infallible Word — and the quiet obedience of His servants.

January 1984

Chapter Two

A President and A Nun

The government has finally admitted what most folks have suspected for a long time: despite decades of extravagant political promises and bloated budgets, the massive bureaucracy called government simply is incapable of solving all (or even most) of America's social ills.

President Reagan made it official in a meeting with religious and business leaders, and later in an address to the nation. The government is tightening its belt, he announced, reducing taxes, expenditures, and abandoning a host of less than effective social programs. "Fill the vacuum," the President challenged us; private groups and volunteer efforts should take over those functions being cut from the budget.

Special interest groups who have lived off the federal largesse for half a century howled like wounded coyotes. Demonstrators organized, the press predicted doom, and Congress shuddered.

But the greatest threat to the President's policies comes not from the obvious assault of powerful lobbies, but from a force much more subtle, and deeply ingrained in our culture. It is what can best be described as the massive impersonalization of American life. Let me explain.

Rapid technological advance, government growth and mass communication's pervasive influence have left individuals feeling helpless, little more than observers of the passing parade. The "real" world is that which flashes across the electron tube each night in the family living room.

Steady erosion of a person's sense of participation has had far-reaching and little understood consequences. If what a person does doesn't matter, why do anything? Or, even worse, why *not* do anything?

Since individuals' actions don't matter, there is no responsibility or accountability. When something goes wrong, it is not "our" fault, it is the "system's." We grow to resent the "system"—that institution we call society—and ultimately, unknowingly, we go to war with ourselves.

Since government has for so long promised to solve all human problems, the citizen sees paying taxes as his sole civic duty. Americans have grown accustomed to believing that the amount withheld from their pay checks satisfies their moral obligation to their neighbors, particularly to the less fortunate. That is why, though we may grumble over high taxes and welfare cheaters, down deep, I suspect, we like the system. After all, it spares us the pain of looking into the vacant eyes of a hungry person, or drying the tears of an abused child. Money is a cheap substitute for human caring.

The Washington press corps virtually ignored the President's comments about volunteerism, feasting instead on the President's budget cuts. In doing so, the press totally missed the point. President Reagan is tackling something much bigger than the budget or the economy.

In asking us to get personally involved, to do something for neighbors in need, he is talking about a reformation in

American life, in how the individual views his role in society.

The Christian church should need no such exhortation from secular government. It should be leading the way, for our Lord has already commanded us to care for the widows and orphans, to feed the hungry, visit the sick and imprisoned, and bear one another's burdens. And it is our great heritage.

Up until this century, evangelicals pioneered schools, built the first hospitals, cleaned up work abuses in the coal mines, provided homes for the poor and orphans, to mention but a few.

And — as so often we discovered when applying biblical teaching — it works! Prison Fellowship now has tens of thousands active volunteers in the United States and overseas. They are alive and vibrant, full of purpose and excitement. *They are participants, and they are making a difference.* Prisoners are being changed and so are prisons — institutions in which government has an almost unblemished record of failures.

In this ministry and others like it we see the gospel demonstrated through human caring. There is a consistent refrain I hear whenever I visit a prison where our volunteers have been at work: "We never knew anyone cared for us," the inmates say, "but now we know someone does. Jesus does and the PF volunteers do — they care — someone cares." Government programs can't do that, but people can.

Even as the President launched his volunteerism campaign from the White House, another world leader spoke on the other side of the Capitol. Mother Teresa had come to the ghetto area of Southeast Washington, known as Anacostia, to open a convent for nine Sisters of Charity. The press crowded into a church hall to interview the ninety-pound Albanian woman whose worn, shriveled face speaks of the countless thousands of sick and dying she has cared for in Calcutta.

"Why don't you use your influence to start a government program?" one reporter asked. "You could help so many more people that way." Mother Teresa patiently replied that her call is to help people, not begin programs.

That is a baffling notion in a city like Washington, which exists to create new programs, start agencies to administer them, and sell newspapers that report about them. Instead of pleading for government grants to combat poverty, Mother Teresa and her Sisters moved into a neighborhood to share it— and to care. They understand the deep spiritual union of what Paul called the "fellowship of suffering." Unfathomable to a skeptical press corps, it is that fellowship which draws us close to our Lord, who suffered for us.

Mother Teresa's message is plain enough: "Do something for someone else ... something that goes beyond the realm of a gift, and into the category of a sacrifice ... for the sick, unwanted, crippled, heartbroken, aged or alone."

Though they come from two different worlds, each in their own way, the President of the United States and the nun from Calcutta are giving us the same message. It is prophetic, unsettling, even threatening. And we should be grateful that it is.

November 1981

Chapter Three

A Movement, Not a Monument

Just before the dedication of our new general offices, an old friend congratulated me. "This is God's blessing," he said excitedly, "and proof of your success!"

It *is* a blessing — and we are profoundly grateful. The DeMoss House's warmth and openness stand as a powerful statement to the world that Christians are taking to heart their Lord's command to care for "the least of these."

But is our new property proof of our success? No, I believe that line of thinking is one of the sad delusions of the church today.

For many, church growth has become the goal, larger and more elaborate sanctuaries the measure of spirituality. Pastors who are proven church builders are pursued like pro athlete draft choices; for many the bids include six-figure incomes.

This "bigger is better" mindset is deadly. Vernon Grounds has wisely warned, "We are sinfully concerned with bigness — with budgets, buses, buildings and baptisms."

A sure cure for that "sinful concern" is a visit to Europe's huge cathedrals — or its sparsely attended parish churches. Inspired architecture does not change lives; nor do big buildings impart spiritual power.

And the church is not a building anyway. The New Testament describes it not as a place, but a people: the "holy nation," the "Body of Christ," the "people of God's own choosing." Paul writes, "By one Spirit we were baptized into one body." The church, then, is you and me — God's people. An organism, not an organization; a movement, not a monument.

This was brought home to me during an unforgettable experience a few years ago. During a visit to London I asked a friend to take me to Clapham, the village where William Wilberforce lived almost two centuries ago. Wilberforce was the Christian member of Parliament who led the twenty-year fight, ultimately victorious, against the slave trade. He is one of my great heroes.

Wilberforce was joined by a small band of like-minded Christians who lived, worked and prayed together in the Clapham home of Henry Thornton.

We drove one night through London's crowded streets past block after block of Victorian row houses. A few miles from downtown we came upon a hill, then around a bend. "There it is," my host exclaimed. "That's where Henry Thornton's home used to be!"

"Used to be?" I replied in disbelief. "Surely it has been preserved as an historic site!"

"No," my friend responded, "leveled long ago."

I was stunned. In the U.S., there are markers at the site of obscure battles, even the footprints of screen stars preserved in cement. But here there was nothing.

We drove several blocks to the old church on Clapham Green.

"Wilberforce once preached here," the rector told me proudly, pointing to a painting in the center of the stained glass behind the altar — a "quite good likeness" of Wilberforce. I squinted but could barely make it out.

"Is that all there is?" I asked, my disappointment deepening. "Oh, no," he replied, leading me to a small brass plaque and a pile of booklets about Wilberforce under a sign, "50 p each." That was it.

We left the church and walked across Clapham Green. "After all these men accomplished," I mumbled, "surely more could have been done to honor them." But suddenly I stopped and stared across the soft grass. In my mind's eye I could see row upon row of men and women, freed from the laden slave ships; I could even hear the clanging chains falling from their arms and legs.

Of course, of course, I thought. Clapham is just what Wilberforce and his colleagues would want. No spires of granite or marble, no cold statues and lifeless buildings. Rather, the monument to Wilberforce is the legacy of countless millions, once enslaved, who today live in freedom.

So, as we joyfully dedicated our new PF home and broke ground for our new offices, it was with the lesson of Wilberforce in mind. We thank God for granting us this place through the generosity of so many faithful friends. We commit ourselves to be good stewards of the property and gifts with which we've been entrusted.

But within our joy is the sober reminder that buildings are not eternal. Buildings are not the Body of Christ. Our standard is not earthly success, but faithfulness to God's calling.

Like the God-ordained work of Wilberforce and his friends, the success of this ministry is to be measured not by the size or beauty of its buildings, but by the holy things which happen within them. May it be that when people generations hence look upon this ministry, they will see not a collection of handsome monuments in Reston, Virginia, but rather living monuments around the world — men and women free from the chains of prison and sin.

March 1985

Chapter Four

On Christianity and Magic Wands

A few months ago I received a troubled letter from a Prison Fellowship volunteer — let's call her Susan. Her letter points to one of the toughest problems in prison ministry — and most of us can empathize.

Susan has been regularly visiting inmates in one of the country's roughest prisons for more than two years. She coordinates volunteers for our seminars, takes parolees into her home, and gives sacrificially. It would be hard to find a more committed supporter of this ministry.

Her letter began with a report on several of the men she was helping. First was Jim, who had been doing well in his walk with Christ, but had slipped back into his old lifestyle of twenty years, homosexuality. Susan asked for prayer. Then there was Harry — back on drugs; and Bill, dabbling in alcohol again; and Barry, continuing to lose control of his violent temper.

All these men, Susan explained, had given their lives to Christ — they were sincere — but still, problems and failures and struggles. They were taking their toll on Susan. "Sometimes," she wrote, "I feel so very overwhelmed...how can I tap the Lord's power? Jesus is the victor, but where is the victory?"

And she was worried not only about the failures of the men but about her own inadequacies as well. "We're supposed to get hold of the same resurrection power that brought Jesus back to life...what's wrong?" she asked.

The frustration of even mature believers like Susan is not hard to understand. Everything in our society is measured by the "bottom line": the results. Success is all that counts; we have become an impatient and intolerant people.

That secular mentality has insidiously infiltrated and influenced our theology — much of today's teaching and preaching communicates Christianity as an instant fix to all of our pains and struggles. Consequently, we begin to think of our faith as a sparkling magic wand: we wave it, and presto, our problems are gone in a puff of smoke.

But this is, bluntly put, heresy. Like most subtle heresies, it tickles our ears. It sounds so easy, and its appeal, particularly in this egocentric age, is also that it tells us what we want to hear: how to get what we want.

But at the same time it takes an awful toll. It not only makes Christians incredibly naive in approaching complex problems, but it can shatter the fragile faith of the believer who expects the magic wand to work every time. When those problems don't disappear, when ministry isn't just a snap of the fingers, he questions whether his spirituality is faulty. The result is guilt — and that clouds the believer's vision and withers the spirit.

If we trust this fairy-tale brand of Christianity, we eventually will fall victim to its consequent paralysis. Certainly as we confront our own repeated sins and failures, but also as we encounter the stumblings of those to whom we minister.

And their mishaps may well be in areas that we cannot understand or have not experienced. Many inmates come from years of incarceration — crushing tedium with its flares of sudden violence — an ugly gray world of confines, bars, cells. Others struggle with lifelong drug dependence, alcohol addiction. Others come-from broken homes or were abused as children. Many know intimately *deep* brokenness and rejection and failure that most volunteers may have experienced only superficially.

In fact, considering the hostile reality of prison, the miracle is that so many do live for Christ behind bars, and then go on to make it on the outside. The more our ministry spreads, the more we see it happen — the gospel *does* change lives.

But it is in God's timing, not ours. And it is the result of His sovereign will, not of any magic wands we may think we wield.

So we learn to work with patience, love, understanding, forgiveness and perseverance, remembering that for men and women in prison, as for those of us outside, growth is often difficult. Lessons always seem to get learned the hard way. There may be two steps forward for each one back, but it often seems the other way around. And sometimes we don't see any steps forward at all.

The experience of one of Prison Fellowship's Washington seminar grads illustrates this. Recently released from prison, Peter was shopping with his small daughter at a neighborhood store when it was held up. In the resulting confusion he was presented with a temptation — and he gave in. Consequently charged with petty larceny and slammed into jail, he faces another prison term. A heartbreaking failure — but also a sharp lesson. Peter told a PF staffer that God had used the experience to teach him and protect him from establishing a habit pattern —a little wrong here, a bigger one later. He has learned from his error, repented, and walks with renewed conviction.

Peter's story also teaches us. We can't smile blithely, wave our wand, and expect neat rows of squeaky-clean Christian converts. Instead, we must be realistic in our ministry — and that means sharing their sufferings, supporting them in failures and brokenness.

So we'll stand with our brother during the coming months and for as long as it may take, confident that in God's perfect timing he'll make it.

Susan, by the way, understands. Her last letter told of being in prison during the holidays. "All I can do is be with the men, share their pain — just be there."

"Being there" is what matters. That's why our motivation in ministry is as important as our actions. We go into prisons not to claim spiritual prizes or to chalk up our success records, but because we are called by the risen Christ and instructed by His holy Word that in coming to those in prison we are coming to Him.

We carry not a magic wand, but the cross. And we must understand what that cross signifies: suffering, persecutions, seeming failures. Not the success of the world — but the ultimate and far greater reward of God's approval. His "well done, good and faithful servant" depends not on our successes, but on our obedient faithfulness.

February 1982

Chapter Five

In Search of Self

Some months ago a New York woman left her husband, two children, Park Avenue home, and friends to move to Hawaii and work in a candy store. She resisted all pleas to return, on the grounds that selling chocolates was her way of "finding herself."

The wife of a close friend recently abandoned him for the glittering ski slopes of Aspen; again, to "find herself."

Another acquaintance told me how he had "found himself" at an est seminar, where he'd been encouraged to release inner tensions by screaming obscenities at anyone within earshot.

These are not isolated cases. Tragically in fact, they are typical, mere symptoms of fast-spreading crisis. Blessed by unprecedented affluence in the sixties and seventies, Americans rightly concluded there must be more to life than material prosperity, but were beguiled into believing the answers they craved could be found by looking deep enough within. The resultant identity search has paraded under a host of banners: Encounter groups, Eastern cults, est, TM, and a long line of others.

It's an age-old dilemma — one that led Solomon to cry out,

"vanity of vanities!" The search for fulfillment through self-discovery has always been doomed from the beginning.

Why? First, because the human heart is deceitful, impenetrable. We equip ourselves with a variety of protective mechanisms. Psychological studies, for example, show that people consistently rate themselves higher than their peers evaluate them.

Second, what if we do succeed in seeing ourselves for what we are? We come face to face with the evil within, caught in the most deadly predicament of all: the discovery we are trapped by our guilt, with no way to find forgiveness.

Third, a by-product of searching for meaning within the four walls of self is this — the search inevitably excludes the community of which we are a part. Without acknowledging our responsibilities to others, we alienate ourselves. One is reminded of Fritz Perls' poem, a modern credo in the early seventies: "You are you and I am I, and if *by chance* we find each other, it's beautiful." If we understand that implicitly humanist perspective, we know those chances are slim at best.

Many today have picked up the term "secular humanism" and made it their red-flag rallying cry. Some Christians label all that they abhor — abortion, "liberal" politicians, opponents to school prayer, impious lifestyles — as the evils of secular humanism. But that can cause us to miss the real point.

The root issue is that secular humanism by definition recognizes only a godless universe, one limited to the temporal realm of human existence. Since nothing above the human scope exists, one must find ultimate truth in self and human reason.

The consequences are pernicious. If man is but a chance collision of atoms, he has no eternal value. So why not live for the moment? Why not be continually stoned, abandon loved ones to sell chocolates, or express yourself by screaming expletives in your neighbor's ear?

From the beginning, humanist notions have crept into man's theology. Eve succumbed to Satan's temptation that she could, through knowledge, be like God. First-century gnostics claimed they could reach God through the power of reason. That belief has been at the heart of almost every heresy, including today's cheapened gospel that assures us our mental attitude can bring our lives meaning and order.

Just recently I read with sadness an article by a beloved brother which explained his desire to "find himself."

"God gives us freedom to be whatever we like," he wrote. "He gives each of us a unique, authentic self and then encourages us to discover it, nurture it and expose it to others."

God does indeed create us with distinct individuality and gifts. But nowhere have I been able to find the premise in Scripture that He has left us to define what constitutes our personal authenticity. Rather, I find that God has a sovereign plan for our lives which we discover, not in seeking ourselves, but in seeking His will.

Dietrich Bronhoeffer's poem written shortly before his execution by the Nazis expresses the universal dilemma. "Who am I?" he begins, then recounts the perceptions of others: "They tell me I bore the days of misfortune equably, smilingly, proudly ... " But his following verses describe the person he knows within: "restless and longing and sick ... faint, and ready to say farewell to it all."

"Am I one person today and tomorrow another?" Bonhoeffer closes, "Am I both at once? A hypocrite before others, and before myself a contemptible woebegone weakling? Who am I? They mock me, these lonely questions of mine."

His poignant words reveal the essence of the human search. This is why Christ tells us we must lose our life for His sake in order to find it. We discover meaning and purpose not in the search for self, but in surrender of self, in obedience to

Christ. In right relationship with our Creator, knowing we belong to Him, we pour ourselves out in service to others.

The concluding line of Bonhoeffer's poem captures that ultimate answer, the only hope in the search for self: "Whoever I am, Thou knowest, O God, I am Thine!"

September 1982

Chapter Six

The Problem of Power

After my speech to a large evangelical convention, a secular reporter asked, "Doesn't the Bible teach born-again Christians to be loving and humble?"

"Of course," I replied.

"Well," he continued, "I've toured the convention displays, and the bigger the exhibit, the more arrogant I've found the people running it. Why?"

Though I defended my brethren, I knew there was truth in the reporter's barbed question. It is heady stuff to reach by TV into millions of living rooms — or to run big staffs and multi-million-dollar operations. That is power. And power can — yes, even among Christians — breed arrogance.

Worldly power is not inherently evil, but it is inherently corrupting. I saw how the White House transformed young political idealists into prideful "supermen," myself included. The same thing can happen to the prestige-conscious businessman, the bullying shop steward, the dominating parent.

The problem of power is especially important for evangelical

Christians this year (1984). For with polls showing more than fifty million born-again Americans, politicians are openly courting evangelicals: President Reagan, for example, kicked off his re-election campaign with a Bible-quoting speech to Christian broadcasters.

This newfound political muscle should be good news, enabling us to restore morality to government, reverse the surging tides of apostasy.

But there is a problem, one I saw from the other side. One of my assignments in the Nixon White House was liaison with special interest groups, including religious. I arranged cruises on the Presidential yacht for prominent clergymen, Oval Office sessions for evangelical leaders.

The religious leaders got the chance to make their points with the President — though most were so in awe they didn't — but most important, those meetings paid off handsomely on election day. Religious leaders, I discovered, were the most naive about politics.

It's easy to become enthralled with access to places of supposed power. In time, however, without even knowing it, our well-intentioned attempts to influence government can become so entangled with a particular political agenda that it becomes our focus; our goal becomes maintaining our political access. When that happens, the gospel is held hostage to a political agenda — and we become part of the very system we were seeking to change.

Friedrich Nietzsche, the nineteenth-century philosopher who well understood the dark side of power, once wrote, "Be careful when you fight the dragon, lest you become a dragon."

So do we retreat from the political arena? Of course not. John Calvin argued the "cultural imperative," the need for Christians to make an impact in all areas of life; that includes politics.

The real question, then, is how do we reconcile the corrupting nature of power with our cultural imperative?

First, politicians lead us to believe that there are political
solutions to all our ills. That is an illusion; and if we are taken
in by it, it will distract us from the real problems — which are at
their root spiritual.

Second, those involved in politics need to heed Plato's
words, "Only those who do not desire power are fit to hold it."
This is radically opposed to the self-aggrandizing nature of
our political system, but there is special wisdom in this for
the Christian. For we are taught that to lead, we must serve; the
call to political leadership is not one of greater self-advance-
ment, but of greater death of self — in service to others.

Third, Christians need to define the real objective. The late
scholar, and my beloved friend, Fran Schaeffer, summed it
up: "The goal for the Christian is not power, but justice...God
in His sheer power could have crushed Satan in his revolt ...
Instead ... Christ died that justice, rooted in what God is,
would be the solution."

Fourth, Christians need to hold one another accountable.
Though I know intellectually how vulnerable I am to pride and
power, I am the last one to know when I succumb to their
seduction. That's why spiritual Lone Rangers are so dangerous
— and why we must depend on trusted brothers and sisters who
love us enough to tell us the truth.

Fifth, power and authority must not be confused. Power is
the ability to affect one's ends or purposes in the world. Authority is having not only the power (might), but the *right* to affect
one's purpose. Power is often maintained by naked force;
authority springs from a moral foundation. Mother Teresa is
the best living example. She spends her life helping the powerless die with dignity; yet few people command more authority worldwide.

So be not deluded. The evangelical movement *is* gaining power in American life. But that is not a cause of unrestrained rejoicing; rather, it should lead us to some sober soul-searching. For worldly power — whether measured by buildings, budgets, baptisms or access to the White House — is more often the enemy than the ally of godliness.

July 1984

Chapter Seven

Vigilante Violence: Looking for Heroes and Villains

Two stories of violence have dominated recent headlines.

One began in a New York City subway in late December. A shy, balding thirty-seven-year-old electrical engineer, Bernhard Goetz, emptied his .38 caliber pistol point-blank into four teenagers who were, as he put it, "hassling" him for $5. As of this writing, one of the four remains in a coma, paralyzed from the waist down.

The second incident took place in Pensacola, Florida. Two twenty-one-year-olds, Matt Goldsby and James Simmons, confessed to the Christmas day bombing of three abortion clinics. Goldsby's fiancée and Simmons' wife were also implicated. Devout church members, all four said they acted on religious convictions. No one was hurt in the bombings.

I am deeply opposed to blowing up abortion clinics, just as I am to gunning down menacing strangers in the subway. I hasten to point this out at the outset lest some readers fail to read this piece through to its conclusion.

These two cases are similar. Goetz was mugged a few years

ago, repeatedly complained about the ineffectiveness of the police, and, though denied a gun permit, began to carry a .38. Goldsby and his friends felt increasingly helpless as legal slaughter continued day after day at local abortion clinics. The young Christians' consciences burned.

In both cases frustration ripened into anger, then erupted into violence against the evils Goetz and Goldsby believed could be stopped no other way. Both, tragically misguided, took the law into their own hands; in that sense, both are vigilantes.

But the public's reaction to the two cases has been strikingly different. Overnight, Goetz became a folk hero. Along New York's East River Drive appeared a huge hand-painted sign: "Power to the vigilante — NY loves ya!" Someone offered to post the $50,000 bond for Goetz' release from jail. The gun lobby compared him to Charles Bronson, vigilante hero of the film *Death Wish*. "Completely justified," they said as they kicked in several thousand to his fast-growing defense fund. Roy Innis, head of the Congress of Racial Equality, called it "the greatest contribution to crime reduction in the past twenty-five to thirty years."

Opinion surveys also revealed overwhelming public support. The response of a fifty-seven-year-old secretary was typical: "It should happen more often." A lawyer friend of mine wished he had the case. "I'd walk him out of court," he said. "No jury would ever convict."

But Goldsby and his accomplices did not fare so well. They were labeled "terrorists" and "religious fanatics." No defense fund was even proposed; besides, the judge refused bail. So Goldsby sits in jail and will stay there.

Outraged civil liberties groups have led a cacophony of condemnation. "Right to lifers" were quick to disown the young men; one prominent evangelical, an implacable abortion foe, called those who perpetrate such acts "deranged." Arsonists started a fire in the church Goldsby attends, scrawling across the door, "an eye for an eye." The same lawyer friend who boasted he'd walk Goetz out of court said he wouldn't touch this case.

Why has the public made Goetz a hero and Goldsby a villain?

Admittedly, the abortion clinics were operating according to the law (whether one likes it or not), while the subway hoodlums were — if Goetz' allegations are true — acting unlawfully. And Goetz is arguing self-defense, but that is shaky at best: two of the boys were shot in the back, apparently fleeing. So in New York a young man — if he survives — is crippled for life.

I believe the real reason for the inconsistent public response is simply this: Abortion, in the public mind, is not a personal threat. After all, we've been born — which means we survived nine months in our mothers' wombs without being torn limb from limb by a pair of forceps or poisoned by a saline solution. The public is not personally endangered by abortion; thus the condemnation for those who resort to violence to stop it.

But being mugged is an immediate, deeply felt *personal* danger — particularly for the millions of New Yorkers who must descend each day into the underworld of their subway system. Fear of crime is real; thus the applause for those who resort to violence to stop it.

The public reaction to these two tragedies exposes a disturbing truth about ourselves. We make moral judgments based not on any absolute value structure (which for the Christian is the revelation of the sovereign God), but on the basis of what affects us personally. And that relativism is a far more insidious danger than subway shootings or abortion clinic bombings. It is the supreme expression of the egocentricity which grips American culture today.

The perpetrators in these cases will be punished—Goldsby for sure and perhaps Goetz as well. We hope Goetz' paralyzed victim will survive. But the real question is, can law and order survive in a land where justice is determined not by moral principle but by personal expediency?

February 1985

Chapter Eight

Watergate Revisited

Dubious though it is to celebrate the anniversary of a burglary —a bungled one at that—that is just what the media did this past month. For weeks I was pursued by a bevy of reporters, all wanting reflections on Watergate a decade later.

Three main questions surfaced repeatedly. And interestingly enough, from them emerged one of the great themes of the gospel.

First: "Could Watergate happen again?"

A surprising number of Americans seem to have the utopian idea that by throwing one bunch of rascals out of office we cleanse the system of corruption forever. But the naiveté of that belief is exposed by events of the past decade. Consider the government scandals in India, Israel, Japan, West Germany. And as the cast of Watergate villains languished in prison, some of their successors were found accepting lavish favors from Korean businessmen, others busily dispensing illegal prescriptions for narcotics in the White House basement, and still others taking wads of cash from FBI agents disguised as Arab sheiks.

What has changed since the Fall? The wrenching dilemma of

the human spirit is captured in the anguished words of the great apostle: "The good that I wish I do not do; but I practice the very evil that I do not wish."

Like Paul, I have known the awful grip of evil and the insidious way it can masquerade as virtue. His words remind us that man is, by his very nature, a sinner, incapable of restraining his own sin. It's the most fundamental proposition of Judeo-Christian belief.

That is not to say that all men will breach their public trust, as we did; but Watergate was a manifestation of the innate evil within — and therefore, of course, it could happen again.

The second question generally dealt with me: "Aren't you bitter? What are your regrets?"

Just as Watergate demonstrated the corruption of man, so it helped show me my desperate need for God. It led me to Romans 8, where Paul provides the answer to the tormented cry of the human soul evoked in chapter 7: it is in Christ Jesus that we are set free.

Bitter? Never.

Sure, Watergate caused my world to crash around me and sent me to prison. I lost many of the mainstays of my existence —the awards, the six-figure income and lifestyle to match, arguing cases in the highest courts, a position of power at the right hand of the President of the United States. But only when I lost them did I find a far greater gain: knowing Christ. I learned the truth of Jesus' words, "He who wishes to save his life shall lose it. But whoever loses his life for My sake shall find it."

That paradox is an impenetrable mystery for the secular mind—but the cardinal truth of the Christian faith.

And I can say, as did Solzhenitsyn, bless you, prison, for having been in my life. For there I caught a glimpse of God's view of His world and His passion for justice and righteousness.

In prison I realized how preoccupation with self had blinded me; when the scales fell from my eyes, I saw how inverted my own values had been.

When I was in the White House I viewed justice as a majority vote, fifty percent plus one. It was simply the law, which I tried to influence for those whose power, position or campaign contribution was significant enough to get my single-minded attention.

Justice was also the instrument for punishing and removing from society those who did not live by the rules that people like me set up. But from my prison cell I saw people serving long years for trivial offenses. I found young men who couldn't retain prestigious attorneys, others who couldn't afford any lawyer at all. I knew people who were sentenced without knowing why — or for how long. I began to see why God has always spoken through the perspective of the powerless, why He makes special demands on His people to care for the oppressed, sick and suffering. I learned to see justice not in relation to human institutions and laws, but in terms of the righteousness of God and His Word.

Regrets? No. I'm grateful to God — and eternally so.

The third question was invariably the same: "What should be the lessons of Watergate?"

If man is corrupt and Christ's redeeming power is the only rescue, then we as a nation and as individuals will never be saved by intrinsically sinful human governments. Watergate should make us skeptical — but not with a cynicism that scoffs, "All politicians are alike, so we can't trust any." Such a nihilistic view leads only to a destruction of all authority.

No, I speak of a different skepticism. It is based on a healthy realism about man and his institutions — and the solid assurance of God's grace. British writer Harry Blamires summed it up well: "Secular skepticism about our civiliza-

tion is [not] by any means the same thing as Christian skepticism about it. The former tends to breed despair. The latter
is rooted in hope, for it is grounded in awareness of God ...
Secular skepticism about the world is wholly negative, for it
opens no doors and offers no comfort ... Christian skepticism
is a by-product of faith and hope in another order that can
itself transform this one."

Watergate's lessons ought to remind us of who we are —
and who He is. And that should not make us cynics, but should
drive us into the arms of the living God. If so, Watergate's
anniversaries should always be occasions to sing anew the
words of the Psalmist: "It is better to take refuge in the Lord
than to trust in princes."

July 1982

A Church in Need of Healing

We recently wrote Prison Fellowship supporters who hadn't contributed in several years to ask why they had stopped. We wanted to find out what people thought of us.

Replies ran the gamut, including notes from those who had simply forgotten, and sent in much-appreciated checks. Some voiced criticism, which was also welcome. We learn from it.

One letter raised a point which illustrates a basic problem in the church today. The pastor of a big city church wrote, "We used to contribute because we believe in your prison work, but we couldn't keep giving after reading your statement of faith. Our denomination does not subscribe to your stand on inerrancy."

I appreciated his honesty, but was also disheartened. The Christian church is full of buzzwords which conjure up all sorts of preconceived images. The moment a word like inerrancy is uttered, lights flash, alarms sound and the person using it is labeled, indexed and sorted into an appropriate box. Sometimes I think the church is like a huge complex of separate rabbit warrens into which each leader nervously herds his faithful followers to keep them away from other rabbits.

As soon as we categorize our fellow-Christians, we effectively block all communication. Any husband and wife who don't communicate are headed straight for divorce court. It is the same with the church.

Most historians trace the major schism in today's church to the late 1800s when evangelical leaders, convinced of Jesus' imminent return, concentrated the work of the church on saving souls. Other Christians, who interpreted the concern with evangelism as indifference to human suffering, began to concentrate on social missions. Over the years the gulf widened and mistrust grew. Nonevangelicals turned away from "soul-winning" more and more, while evangelicals began to see "social action" as a red-flag label.

How supremely ironic. For it was evangelicals who led the massive social reforms of the late nineteenth century — cleaning up abuses in the coal mines, pioneering child labor laws, introducing public education and public hospitals, and abolishing the slave trade. That is social action! But when we allow ourselves to be trapped by stereotypes, we evangelicals all but disown our own proud heritage.

Christians on both sides are usually careful to protect themselves from theological contamination. So they remain in their own safe and secure enclaves, associating only with like-minded brethren. But it's amazing what happens when we take down those walls and communicate with one another. I was interviewed recently for a national public broadcasting program by representatives of mainline nonevangelical churches. When we finished, one pastor leaned over to me. "I don't understand it," he said. "I agree with everything you say, but I'm not supposed to ... I mean, you're a conservative, but you talk about justice and social involvement."

How stereotypes blind us!

I believe what I believe. On the matter of inerrancy, for example, my convictions are fervent, the result of a great deal of study and prayer. Yet it would be sheer arrogance for me to cut myself off from those who do not share my views. If I did, there would be little chance I could win them over. A prominent Christian scholar who vehemently opposed biblical inerrancy wrote me that the literature and tapes I had shared with him on the subject had slowly changed his mind. But "convincing" him was a matter of patience and communication, not force.

That was the Apostle Paul's approach to the rampant divisions in the early church. While his letters were forthright, their whole thrust was a loving concern to bring believers out of error and into sound doctrine.

Of course, like Paul, we must recognize clear standards for breaking fellowship — the deity of Christ, for example. But we must be sure when issues divide us that they are irreconcilable essentials.

Three suggestions might help keep us from majoring on minors. First, let's declare a moratorium on labeling. We should be able to listen to one another in love without compromising our convictions. Perhaps we can enlighten one another; certainly we can reaffirm our common beliefs.

Second, we evangelicals must reassert our heritage of biblically-based compassion and social concern. For example, Prison Fellowship has undertaken a number of practical community assistance programs such as our Community Service Projects. By their very nature, these programs have broken down the stereotypical image of evangelical indifference to social concerns, and have been a powerful witness as well.

Third, let's rest our case on the holy Word of God. The more I read Scripture, the more I am driven to care for prisoners, the oppressed, the needy. Ironic, isn't it? My view of an inerrant Scripture, which so offended my friend in New York, is the very thing which compels me to go into the prisons and do the social work he so affirms. We're still corresponding, and he'll make that connection eventually. In fact, his last letter included a gift for the ministry. We have learned to disagree in love.

I sometimes dream of a church healed in love, no longer divided into armed camps, but caring passionately about winning others to Christ *and* striving for the righteousness of God's justice. We have not yet seen what that kind of whole church will do for the needs of this fragmented world.

August 1982

Chapter Ten

Is There Evidence of the Resurrection?

Several months ago I enjoyed a reunion with an old friend, once a Washington journalist, now a full-time novelist. My friend described his spiritual pilgrimage: his coming to terms with God, his growing church involvement, his new perspectives. "But," he interjected, "I'm not sure I can buy the deity of Christ ... I mean, the resurrection."

I know few people with more compassion and decency. If "goodness" were the key to the Kingdom, my writer friend would be far closer to the head of the line than I'll ever be.

But he could not accept the resurrection, without which our faith is, as Paul put it bluntly, "worthless." I argued hard, reviewing many of the historical, scientific and psychological arguments for the case that Christ rose. Though we parted good friends, he was not persuaded.

Ironically, only a few days after our luncheon, during an Easter trip to two Indiana institutions, I saw firsthand evidence that Christ did indeed rise from the tomb. It was not scientific proof, but the far more convincing demonstration of the lives of

men and women — those locked in the hopelessness of prison —
as well as those on the outside. Events in the life of former judge
William Bontrager serve as one very powerful illustration.

Bill Bontrager's story is interwoven with that of Harry
Fred Palmer, a young Vietnam veteran who accepted Christ in
1977 while in jail awaiting sentencing for a string of house
burglaries. His offense carried a mandatory ten to twenty year
sentence in Indiana, though that law, already acknowledged as
harsh, was changed just eighteen days after his arrest.

Judge Bontrager, who had himself been converted to
Christ a year earlier, reviewed Palmer's case carefully. He realized the mandatory ten-year sentence would destroy rather
than rehabilitate Palmer, so he declared it unconstitutional.
Bontrager ordered him to serve one year in the state penitentiary and then, upon release, to reimburse those he had
robbed and provide community service.

Palmer did just that. He was a model prisoner; after release
he was reunited with his wife and family, and began paying
back his victims. The case seemed closed, a model of justice,
restitution and restoration.

But the Indiana Supreme Court swung into action; claim-
ing that Judge Bontrager had erred, they ordered him to send
Palmer back to prison — for at least nine more years!

For Bontrager, the order was clearly a case of choosing
between the law of man and the law of God. He had been reading the Old Testament prophets; the words of Amos seared his
conscience. He knew the Supreme Court's order didn't meet
God's standard of justice and righteousness, but would instead
punish a man twice for the same crime, merely to satisfy a
technicality of the law.

So Bontrager stepped aside, turning the case over to
another judge. A nightmarish sequence of events followed. The
Court slammed Palmer into Westville Correctional Center,

declared Bontrager in contempt, fined him $500, and sentenced him to thirty days in prison. Though that sentence was suspended, proceedings were begun to remove him from the bench. Rather than allow his own case to endanger Palmer's appeals for release, Judge Bontrager resigned.

His resignation was not without cost. Bill Bontrager gave up a comfortable salary, the judgeship he had always wanted, a position of respect. His radical talk about obeying God, not man, raised eyebrows in his community as well; so it wasn't as if he left his post in a blaze of glory to open a lucrative law practice. In fact, clients for his small firm have been very scarce. But, as his wife told me, "We are waiting on the Lord to provide — so we're learning patience ... if only we could encourage the phone company and a few other creditors to be patient too!"

So it was that I invited private citizen, ex-judge Bill Bontrager and his wife to accompany me to services at Westville on Easter morning. Bontrager said nothing as we waited for guards to unlock the entrance to the auditorium, but as the steel doors swung open he bolted ahead of me and made his way into the crowd of waiting inmates. Seconds later he found Harry Fred Palmer — and the tall, lanky ex-judge embraced the young ex-burglar in prison denims, as tears rolled down their cheeks.

As I watched their reunion, the witness was clear: a man giving up a respected, comfortable life to fight for what is right, against the inexorable processes of an often hostile world, is evidence that Christ lives. If Christians followed the teachings of a benign dead man, their lives would display an innocuous piety. But when Christians stand up for righteousness and justice, they evidence the power of the living God.

As he would be the first to point out, Bill Bontrager is no saint. He's a country boy at heart who wears cowboy boots and string ties. He makes mistakes. But those who testify for Christ are not perfect people. If they were, one of His mightiest witnesses, a rough fisherman named Peter, would never have been called to serve. But Peter saw the resurrected Christ — and his life revealed that truth. As we see Christ today, our actions, too, will bear witness. The world doesn't need to be convinced by technical arguments that Jesus rose from the dead, but by the evidence of Christians obeying the living Christ within them.

I wish my novelist friend could have been with me on that Easter morning, for none of us who watched Bontrager and Palmer, brothers embracing in a modern-day tomb, could doubt that Jesus — the Prisoner who was executed — rose from His tomb and lives today.

June 1982

Chapter Eleven

Crown Him Lord of All

It's Christmas time again.

This month, as Americans bustle to shopping centers and holiday parties, the strains of a familiar hymn are sure to fill the air. "O come let us adore Him," we will sing heartily, "Christ the Lord."

But do we realize what we're singing? Or are the words so familiar they've lost their real meaning?

"Jesus is Lord." This confession is one of the oldest Christian creeds. By it, New Testament believers submitted themselves to Christ and proclaimed Him ruler of the world. And in doing so they put their lives on the line, the earthly "lords" of their day being most anxious to feed the followers of another Lord to the lions.

Down through the centuries the Christian assertion by word and deed that *Christ is Lord* has been the chief cause of hostility to the gospel. Today that resistance is not less, simply more subtle; secular society seeks to reduce Christianity to a private affair, thus neutralizing it completely. This becomes evident in campaign debates over religion and politics: most Americans, polls tell us, buy the proposition that religion is a personal matter having little effect on the way one lives.

New York Governor Cuomo eloquently advanced this view in a speech at the University of Notre Dame. A practicing Roman Catholic, Cuomo said he fully accepted his church's view on abortion. But, as a public official in a pluralistic society, he could not *force* those views on others. So far so good.

But what's more, the governor continued, he was under no obligation to personally oppose legalized abortion as long as the majority of the people favored it.

So a Christian can adhere to particular beliefs on Sundays, but go along with the crowd the rest of the week, feeling free to act in opposition to his own religious "convictions"?

It's understandable that the secular press hailed Governor Cuomo's speech as brilliant; it rationalized the sticky abortion issue, let some prominent press-favored politicians off the hook, and brushed Christianity aside as publicly irrelevant.

But the speech was also a devastating denial of the Lordship of Christ. With this the prevailing mindset of our culture, it is no wonder that religion seems to be having so little effect on American life. The late George Gallup, Sr. discovered the most bewildering paradox: Religious interest is growing at an unprecedented rate, he said, but so is immoral behavior. Gallup's poll revealed *"little difference between those who go to church and those who don't."*

The greatest challenge facing the church today is to reassert the Lordship of Christ. For as the early Christians knew, and upon which fact they staked their lives, the Scriptures make clear the totality of Christ's claims upon us: "If any man will come after Me, let him deny himself, pick up his cross and follow." Paul describes Jesus as the "only sovereign, the King of kings and Lord of lords." The Word tells us that Jesus became

God incarnate — the One before whom all peoples must one day stand in judgment and whose Lordship every tongue will confess.

If we really understand what being Christian means — that this Christ, the living God, actually comes in to rule one's life — then everything must change: values, goals, priorities, desires and habits. If Christ's Lordship does not disrupt our own lordship, then the reality of our conversion must be questioned.

Let me give you a good example of what happens when Christ is truly Lord. After Jack Eckerd, founder of the Eckerd drugstore chain, committed his life to Christ, he walked through one of his stores and saw with new eyes the magazine racks full of glossy copies of *Playboy* and *Penthouse*. Though retired from active management, he called his president and urged him to clean out the magazines. Management protested: the sales accounted for substantial profits. Though as the largest stockholder Eckerd himself stood to lose money as well — a lot of money — he persisted.

And he prevailed. *Playboy, Penthouse* and their ilk were removed from all 1,700 Eckerd drugstores. And Jack Eckerd has since begun a quiet campaign to get other retail stores to do the same.

When I asked Jack, now a member of Prison Fellowship's Board, what motivated him, he answered simply, "God wouldn't let me off the hook." The most learned theologian couldn't give us a more eloquent description of the Lordship of Christ in action.

As I walked through an Eckerd Drug Store last week, I couldn't help but think about Governor Cuomo's speech when I saw the magazine racks. They wouldn't have been free from smut, I realized, if Jack Eckerd had fallen for the kind of insipid "religion" the governor preached.

Most of us don't influence the corporate decisions of

multimillion dollar companies, but Jack Eckerd's story suggests a simple and practical formula that applies to all of us. Look at your home, business, school, community, politics, through the eyes of Christ. When you see something that isn't right — and you will — don't shrug, blame somebody else, and retreat from the fray. Do something about it!

For such obedience to Christ is the only thing that will put real heart in our familiar Christmas carols this season. Joy to the world — the Lord *is* come!

December 1984

Chapter Twelve

God Isn't Dead, Just Sick and Feeble

For more than a year now, a book by a once obscure rabbi, Harold Kushner, has dominated the best seller lists. Appealingly titled *When Bad Things Happen to Good People*, nearly 500,000 hardcover copies are in print: the soon-to-be released paperback edition is expected to sell in the millions.

The book deals with a familiar query: how can a loving God allow such terrible suffering and evil in the world? It's an age-old question, whether we think of the ancient slaughter of the Cannanites or the horrors of the Holocaust.

Drawing from his own experience — his son died at age 14 of a tragic illness — Kushner answers that God is indeed all-loving, but He is not all-powerful; the bad things which happen are simply out of His control. The rabbi writes, "I can worship a God who hates suffering but cannot eliminate it more easily than I can worship a God who chooses to make children suffer and die."

Obscure no longer, Kushner is big on the celebrity circuit. *Time, Family Weekly, Redbook* and scores of newspapers and magazines have printed interviews and excerpts from his book.

He's steadily flooded with fan mail; one grateful reader wrote, "Maybe now I can believe in a *more realistic* God."

Well, it's nice that Rabbi Kushner can comfort so many Americans. But wait a minute ... What do we mean, a *more realistic* God? Who decides whether God is realistic?

That, of course, is the rub. The god Kushner writes about is neither omnipotent nor sovereign, and is, therefore, not the Creator God of Abraham, Isaac and Jacob, not the all-powerful God revealed in the Holy Bible. Yet people gobble up the book, clamoring for this impotent god.

It is not surprising, I suppose. People yearn for keys to life's mysteries; when someone comes along with an easy answer that gives comfort and rationalizes the supernatural, they stampede the bookstores. We'll sacrifice truth to our own prejudices any day.

But what *is* surprising — shocking is a better world — is not the secular reaction to Kushner's book, but the Christian response. Incredibly, the book has been endorsed by a well-known pastor and by a respected seminary professor, is recommended to the readers of at least one leading Christian journal, and is sold in many Christian bookstores.

Are we blind to what is happening? The waves of secular thinking which crash over us are washing away the very foundations on which the church stands. Hundreds of thousands, including church members and evangelicals, are reading Kushner's book; it is directly shaping people's perception of God. Do we just yawn, roll over, and pull up the covers?

Kushner's simple message, by the way, is not original. For sixty years, "process" theology, so-called, has been spreading like a cancer through the church, dismissing the power of God as noncrucial. "The goodness of God is more important," says John Cobb, a leading process theologian. So God isn't dead, as the liberals of the early sixties argued; now, they say, He's just sick and feeble.

Why do heresies like this flourish? A chief reason is biblical ignorance and disbelief. Despite the ballyhooed "born again" movement, belief in the Bible is declining dangerously. Gallup reports that in 1963, 63 percent of all Americans believed the Bible was the actual Word of God, "to be taken literally"; today only 37 percent do.

Moreover, the church has a woefully inadequate understanding of evil. Because the origin of evil — and why God permits it — is such a hard question we tend to avoid it, as well as its corollary issue, sin. (Are there really any "good" people, as Kushner postulates? If we think so, then we aren't reading our Bibles thoroughly.) Besides, sin and evil aren't popular sermon topics — congregations get offended, uncomfortably convicted, in fact.

A weary and frustrated people are easy prey for those who peddle simple answers to life's toughest questions. But be not confused. The biblical truth is that sin is real and it comes from man; God, on the other hand, is both good *and* all-powerful. His goodness is established beyond all dispute by the fact He allowed His sinless Son to die on the cross for our sin; His omnipotence is affirmed by His victory over sin and death through Christ's resurrection.

That is not an easy answer; it may not even seem fair or "realistic." But as Christians we believe it is true, a fact of history.

The very popularity of Rabbi Kushner's book should wake us up. If simple-sounding pop answers wrapped in the cloak of religious truth are so widely accepted — by unquestioning believers and nonbelivers alike — then we as Christians aren't doing our job. We need to rouse ourselves, take our stand on the holy Word of God, and label heresy as heresy. If we don't proclaim the Truth, who will?

There's no better time to begin than now.

March 1983

Chapter Thirteen

A Case of Moral AIDS

A favorite pastime during my years in government was collect-ing silly political statements. It's a good hobby because there's an endless supply; I've collected some classics.

But Assistant Press Secretary Larry Speakes topped them all when he declared, in the midst of 1984's campaign fervor, "The President will not balance the budget on the backs of the American people."

Twenty years ago, "We won't balance the budget on the backs of the poor" was a popular rallying cry. Then it was farm workers, minorities, the elderly. But now in one grand, mag-nanimous gesture, Speakes included everyone: "... not on the backs of the American people."

Reporters nodded dutifully and wrote down Speakes' every word. *Newsweek* printed the statement as a serious cam-paign pledge. Network anchors repeated it without so much as a wry smile.

Amazing! Have we become so accustomed to absurdity that we accept it as the norm? Maybe so in campaign rhetoric, which bombards us with so many inanities the only defense is to disengage our minds. But tragically, the same stupor seems to be paralyzing our moral sensibilities as well. And that's dangerous.

A few months ago a letter appeared in Ann Landers' newspaper column from a young man brimming with indignation. His girlfriend, after discontinuing her birth control pills without his knowledge, had gotten pregnant. "Some women cannot be trusted," he concluded angrily.

As I read his letter I shook my head. Sadly, so many consider sex outside of marriage an unquestioned right. Maybe, I thought, Ann's response would set him straight.

But her answer virtually endorsed his attitude: "Your letter should be discussed in all high school classrooms in America ... [It] makes abundantly clear that a conniving (or careless) girl can make a tremendous difference in a man's life."

I almost crumpled the paper. No mention of moral right or wrong, just commiseration and the shocking proposal that all high schoolers be taught how to be promiscuous safely.

And in the next letter in her column that day (about a totally different subject), Ann concluded, "May the good Lord continue to bless you." So in one breath this popular counselor gives advice offensive to the living God — and in the next gushingly calls Him up to bless her next correspondent.

Confident of public shock over Landers' advice, we called her office — which reported she had received not one letter of protest!

Where is our sense of outrage? Perhaps our moral sensibilities have been dulled because of today's dazzling instant communications. We sit mesmerized in front of our TVs, unable to turn the sets off, so we turn our minds off instead.

Over time, so much trash is heaped upon us that we come to expect and accept it; the bizarre becomes commonplace. Morally exhausted, we lose our capacity to discern good from evil.

The brilliant essayist Charles Krauthammer, citing economist Thomas Sowell, sums up our predicament beautifully: "The inability to make moral distinctions is the AIDS of the intellectuals: an acquired immune deficiency syndrome ... moral blindness of this caliber requires practice. It has to be learned."

In a culture infected with moral AIDS, words lose all meaning; or, they are manipulated to obscure meaning. Thus taxes become "revenue assessment enhancements"; perversion is "gay"; murder of unborn children is "freedom of choice"; Marxism in the church is called "liberation theology." These are all good words (in the Nazi era "the final solution" had a nice ring to it also). And everyone just nods unquestioningly.

But when words lose their meaning, it is nearly impossible for the Word of God to be received. If sin and repentance mean nothing, then God's grace is irrelevant. Our preaching falls on deaf ears.

This moral deafness leads to disaster. The Scriptures tell us it was when people accepted King Ahab's gross evils as "trivial" that fearsome judgment befell ancient Israel.

Certainly evil is to be expected in a fallen world. What is not expected is for a holy people to accept it. If Christ is Lord of all, Christians must recapture their sense of moral outrage.

When I get upset about issues like the amorality of Ann Landers' column or politicians' flim-flam rhetoric, friends often chide me. "Why bother?" they ask. "That's just the way things are."

But I think of the old story about the man who tried to save Sodom from destruction. The city's inhabitants ignored him, then asked mockingly, "Why bother everyone? You can't change them."

"Maybe I can't change them," the man replied, "but if I still shout and scream it's to prevent them from changing me!"

So I keep screaming.

April 1985

Chapter Fourteen

"The Church Should Mind Its Own Business"

The Senate debate over school prayer was big news last month. Night after night, the networks covered prayer vigils on Capitol Hill, the President's appeal to the nation, heated exchanges between Senators.

But almost obscured by the national furor over the constitutional amendment was a case in an Oklahoma courtroom, the outcome of which could have far greater consequences for religious liberty and the church in America.

The case grew out of the actions of a small church in rural Oklahoma. Some months ago, the elders confronted one of their members, Marian Guinn, who was having an affair with a local man. She was counseled to repent or the church would withdraw from her. Guinn did not deny the charge — her affair was well-known — but, according to the elders, refused to repent.

What does a church do with a member who persists in flagrant sin? The Bible gives clear direction: Paul instructed the church at Corinth to expel members for sexual immorality and told Timothy the rebuke must be public "so that others may take warning." Of course, every effort ought to be made to gently bring offending members around; in this case the elders believed they had exhausted every effort, having confronted Ms. Guinn privately several times. So they applied the strict standards of the Scriptures. (Since the facts are still in dispute as of this writing, I can pass no judgment on whether the elders acted precipitously.)

So Marian Guinn was separated from fellowship. She was also enraged. "What I do or do not do is between God and myself," she said, charging that the elders had no right "to mess with someone's life."

And she promptly hired an attorney who sued the church for more than a million dollars, charging invasion of privacy. Incredibly, to my way of thinking, the court rejected motions to dismiss, thereby asserting jurisdiction over what has always historically been a matter of church business.

The trial began in mid-March; and, incredibly again, the court ruled in Marian Guinn's favor, awarding her $400,000. (The verdict will be appealed.)

The case presents two issues of enormous significance:

The first is whether the state can hold the church liable for enforcing biblical standards on its members. The trial court's decision, if it stands, would be an outrageous invasion by the state in the affairs of the church, and would reduce the church to nothing more than a Sunday morning Rotary Club.

The second issue is less obvious, but even more disturbing — for the Guinn case tells us how the church is perceived by the culture.

Guinn's lawyers argued that their client's love affair was "irrelevant" to the church. Most press accounts were sympathetic to Guinn; one national magazine put quotation marks around the word "sin" as if fornication no longer qualified — except to backwards, narrow-minded church folks.

Guinn's attorney brazenly summed it up: "It doesn't matter if she was fornicating up and down the street. It doesn't give [the church] the right to stick their noses in."

As the world sees us, the church has no business being concerned with the moral standards of its members.

Unfair? Or is the world's perception justified by the way we've acted?

To find the answer, we're forced to ask ourselves some tough questions:

Have we become more concerned with enlistment and church membership than demanding righteousness and spiritual discipline?

Do we preach a prosperity gospel, or do we call our comfortable congregations to repentance?

Do we really insist that our faith make a difference in how we live — including not just piety but our views on justice, caring for the disadvantaged, even our perceptions of art, literature, music?

If we're honest, we have to admit the world's view of us is not so far from the mark. Our culture doesn't think morality is any of our business because they haven't seen us *make* it our business.

It will be bad news if the court should emasculate the church by holding that it can't enforce biblical standards on its members; but it will be even worse news if it turns out that by ignoring our biblical responsibilities we have done it to ourselves.

The celebrated national prayer debate and the obscure trial in Oklahoma suggest that our priorities are confused. It is incongruous for a nation to seek to restore prayer in its schools while at the same time rejecting holiness in its churches.

April 1984

Chapter Fifteen

The Locked Door

I found myself staring at forty listless inmates. Their expressions reflected that despair I have seen and sensed in prison after prison, country after country.

This night, I was in Cardiff, Wales, visiting at the invitation of Welsh Christians organizing Prison Fellowship. The prison warden had called together everyone who regularly attends chapel so I could meet them on my first visit to his institution.

After my brief remarks, an inmate whose eyes had been fixed on me the whole while walked to the front. He was Jewish by birth, he explained, but had converted to Christianity while in college. "I read the New Testament," he commented, "and it made so much sense to me that I joined the church."

Later dropping out of college, he had drifted into a Bohemian section of London, then into drugs and arrest and finally prison.

It was a familiar tale of lostness and grief, but it included as well a painful reminder of how we well-meaning Christians often fail those in need.

"When I got out of prison the last time," the inmate continued, "I really wanted to go staight. I went for help to the minister of my church, but he only lectured me on how terrible my life had been. Then I found that none of the people in the church would even talk to me."

His face took on a pained expression; there was a deep hurt in his voice. What he was relating was unpleasant for him to remember. "Finally," he went on, "I realized that the church didn't want me — didn't trust me around young people. So I left and tried another church. They didn't want me either. I went back to my old friends. And here I am again, the second time in prison."

When the Welshman concluded, my mind flashed back to another inmate and an all too similar episode in the American Northwest. The American inmate was once a hardened con who'd spent the last twenty years of his life in one of the most miserable penal institutions in the U.S. Two years ago, he was converted to Christ, and subsequently became a Christian leader behind the walls. The pastor of a church nearly forty miles from the prison had become interested in the inmate and aided him in discipleship.

Then, unexpectedly, the inmate gained an early release from prison. His first call after reentering society was to the pastor to whom he'd become so close. "You're out!" the pastor exclaimed. "Well, good luck — hope I'll see you sometime."

End of conversation.

The inmate got the message; he wasn't welcome in *that* pastor's church. It was one thing to be ministered to when tucked away in prison; it was another to be welcomed into a "respectable" congregation.

In think of this tragedy, too, whenever I visit a city and

walk its downtown streets. Often I'll stop by to visit old historic churches in the center of the city, as I did recently with a friend on a trip to the Midwest. We were out for an afternoon walk, and I wanted to show him a particularly beautiful and historic chapel connected to a rescue mission. Its name, as an overhead sign announced, was "Church of the Open Door." Unfortunately, as is so often the case, we couldn't get in—the door was locked. If it weren't so tragic, I suppose that would have been humorous, considering the church's name.

I know the reason for the lock-up of course—vandalism is a tremendous problem in many cities. Yet it still bothers me to find a house of worship closed to passersby. It is the symbolic effect of the church of Jesus Christ locking its doors to anyone who might want to walk in off the streets.

Unfortunately, more than symbolism is involved. Many churches not only lock their doors against vandals, but close their doors to the poor or once rebellious sinners—like ex-cons.

But I wonder. I wonder what Jesus would do if He walked our cities' streets today and found the doors to His church locked to those in dire need.

When He was castigated by the religious authorities of His time for associating — and even seeking out — notorious sinners, Jesus replied, in the full force of His righteousness, "It is not the healthy who need a doctor but the sick. I have come not to call the righteous but sinners."

We Christians need to remember that. We need to ask ourselves whether our churches have become "too good" to deal with the sick and the sinful, too heavenly bound to be of much earthly use to the thieves and harlots with whom our Lord spent so much time in prayer and ministry.

Of course, to do what Jesus commands requires us to take risks. We'll be disappointed, frustrated, betrayed. But that's why Jesus also commands us to count the cost of discipleship to Him. That's what being a Christian is all about.

The church is the visible presence on earth of the living although invisible Christ. But it's harder to tell inmates in prison about the living Christ when they find themselves confronted with locked doors, or rebuke and rejection by Christ's people.

June 1980

Chapter Sixteen

The Stink of Sin

A few months ago Albert Speer was interviewed about his last book on ABC's "Good Morning, America." Speer, the Hitler confidante whose technological genius was credited with keeping Nazi factories humming throughout World War II, in another era might have been one of the world's industrial giants. The only one of twenty-four war criminals tried in Nuremburg to admit his guilt, Speer spent twenty years in Spandau prison.

Interviewer David Hartman referred to a passage in one of Speer's earlier writings: "You have said the guilt can never be forgiven, or shouldn't be. Do you still feel that way?"

I will never forget the look of pathos on Speer's face as he responded: "I served a sentence of twenty years, and I could say 'I'm a free man, my conscience has been cleared by serving the whole time as punishment.' But I can't do that. I still carry the burden of what happened to millions of people during Hitler's lifetime, and I can't get rid of it. This new book is part of my atoning, of clearing my conscience."

Hartman pressed the point. "You really don't think you'll

be able to clear it totally?" Speer shook his head, "I don't think it will be possible."

For thirty-five years Speer had accepted complete responsibility for his crime. His writings were filled with contrition and warnings to others to avoid his moral sin. He desperately sought expiation. All to no avail.

I wanted to write Speer, to tell him about Jesus and His death on the cross, about God's forgiveness. But there wasn't time. The ABC interview was his last public statement; he died shortly after.

As I reflected on the tragedy of Albert Speer's vain search for forgiveness, I received a fascinating report from one of our in-prison seminar instructors.

While conducting a seminar in a penitentiary which provided a guest house for those staying on prison business, Randy shared the quarters one night with a prison psychiatrist who was making one of his periodic visits. When the doctor discovered that Randy was a minister, he began to share his own professional frustrations. "I can cure somebody's madness, but I can't cure his badness," he said. "Psychiatry, properly administered, can turn a schizophrenic bank robber into a mentally healthy bank robber; a good teacher can turn an illiterate criminal into an educated criminal."

As the evening wore on, it became apparent that the psychiatrist was struggling with problems of his own. Shifting uncomfortably in his chair, he recounted a session that day with a man who, while high on angel dust, murdered his own child. "Of course he's depressed," the doctor nearly shouted, "who wouldn't be? But if I had done that, I hope I'd have the courage to do the only honorable thing and kill myself too. Of course," he added quickly, "that's not what I said to my patient." Then he settled back into his chair with a long sigh.

Describing the conversation, Randy wrote, "At this point I

could see how much difference the cross of Jesus Christ makes in how men deal with the trail of broken and destroyed lives they leave behind; and how terribly real sin is, not only to the victim, but also to the perpetrator. Suicide is the only reasonable recourse unless there is real forgiveness. There is no way any of us can live with ourselves, or with others as bad as ourselves, unless the blood of Jesus Christ cleanses us from our guilt and shame. I work daily with those whose crimes are nauseating to any reasonable person. The stink of sin would be unbearable but for the historical reality, the moral reality, of the cross which reduces all of us to the common ground of sinners who are equally deserving of hell and equally needing the mercy of God. And in the cross is redemption."

Randy witnessed to the doctor, who acknowledged that he believed in redemption by the grace of God. He couldn't deny it because he had seen its results in the lives of some inmates. But, sadly, he added, he had not experienced it himself.

We know that the good doctor was wrestling with one of the most excruciating human dilemmas. Billions are caught in the web: they can change anything about their lives — jobs, homes, cars, sometimes spouses — but not moral reality.

And so people face two choices. Overwhelmed by the "stink of sin," as Randy so graphically put it, they are, like Albert Speer, driven obsessively to work for their own absolution. Or, in order to live with themselves, they deny their own sin and guilt, lying to themselves to keep on living.

Man's wrenching desire to find inner peace accounts for the faddish popularity of the consciousness movement. But that only makes matters worse because our real disillusionment sets in when we succeed in learning who we really are.

There is only one way out of the agonizing dilemma. It is not through ourselves, but through the One who took your sins and mine upon Himself on the cross.

I have written much about the need to come to terms with sin, about repentance and Christians' duty to change and live by God's ways. So perhaps it is a good time to remind ourselves that the relationship between man and God is always a two-way street. The corollary to man's repentance is God's grace, His loving forgiveness. Grace is what that singular moment in history at Golgotha is all about. For only through the power of Christ's resurrection can we find the forgiveness which makes life bearable.

December 1981

Chapter Seventeen

Apathy and "Capital Punishment"

James Pangburn, a twenty-one-year-old unemployed landscaper from Rockford, Illinois, pleaded guilty last April to trying to steal a one-ton welder from a leasing company. Pangburn was still growing up, and he got drunk from time to time. Apparently he was drinking the night he tried to steal the welder (how anyone could make off with a one-ton welder is beyond me).

A friend described him as " a little wild," but not a criminal; he had been on probation once for burglary. But his father said he was a "good kid" and was planning to get married and settle down.

Apparently, the judge felt a little prison time would help settle him down, and he sentenced James to one year in the Joliet prison.

Terrified, Pangburn thought about running away. But a woman whose children he had helped talk out of drugs convinced him to do his time. With good behavior he would be home in October; he and his fiancée made plans to be married as soon as he was released.

So, on April 21, James Pangburn turned himself in at the Joliet Correctional Center. Within a couple of days his fianceé began receiving alarming notes. Prison psychologists interviewed Pangburn and recommended transfer to a suicide control unit; the recommendation was ignored.

On April 28, Pangburn wrote his fiancée asking her to call the warden; he was in fear for his life. That very night, the limp body of James Pangburn was found hanging in his cell, a bedsheet tied around his neck. It was the first and last violent act the young man had been involved in.

Before he died, he had hastily scribbled and swallowed a note, "The police killed me Disciples [a prison gang] had key to doors inmates." It was found in his stomach during the autopsy.

The official investigation continues with prison officials denying foul play. But Pangburn's father and friends insist he was not the kind to take his own life. "He was a good kid," his father repeated, "and he was looking forward so much to getting out and getting married."

I wish this were an isolated case, but it isn't. Recently I heard about another young man who was arrested for a traffic violation in Chicago. Since he was driving on a revoked license, the judge set bail at $1,000. The young man could not come up with the cash, so he was taken to the county house of correction to spend the night while friends worked on getting bail. During the night a sheet was thrown over his head. He was punched, kicked and held on the floor as he resisted repeated attempts at homosexual rape; then he was burned repeatedly with lighted cigarettes. He was hospitalized for three weeks. The physical scars have healed, but the emotional trauma will be with him the rest of his life.

A very high percentage, some experts say half, of the young people sent to prisons are homosexually assaulted within the first weeks of incarceration. I have talked firsthand with many victims.

Stories like these are so repulsive I can scarcely think about them without feeling outrage. They intensify my conviction to do something with my life to help eliminate these kinds of horrors.

But even more appalling than these dreadful events is the apparent apathy of the public. These stories — and scores more just like them — have all been well reported. Yet there is little evidence of a public rising up in moral indignation, few demands for reform. Why not?

Part of the explanation may be found in another recent news story about the marketing of a new family game called "Capital Punishment." Instead of buying houses on Boardwalk or collecting $200 for passing "Go," the players are each given four "criminals." The object of the game is to get them past "liberals" and into the electric chair. The first player to execute all four of his criminals wins the game.

The manufacturer advertises it as a way to "allow citizens frustrated by violent crime to punish criminals vicariously." Sales are brisk in more than 400 retail outlets.

"Capital Punishment" can, I suppose, be perversely satisfying. It allows us to fantasize our most vengeful passions and appease the anger and rage we all feel over rising crime rates. It's only a game, you say. But could it be that cases like Pangburn and the young traffic violator in Chicago do the same thing for us, subconsciously pandering to our basest instincts?

St. Augustine once wrote of the good man in Rome who attended a gladitorial contest. At first he shielded his eyes from the horror. But within minutes the roar of the crowd was irresistibly intoxicating and he found himself joining the throngs in the Colosseum, lustily cheering as swords tore open flesh, blood flowed, and men died. There is a wretched evil deep within the best of us.

Could this be why we are so apathetic to cases like Pangburn? May it not be so. I hope and pray our society has not become so sick with anger as to find gratification in the spectacle of nondangerous and frightened boys being raped and murdered. Yet I wonder. Why else is the public not so horrified, its conscience so offended that it refuses to permit this travesty to continue?

The leadership, I am convinced, must come from those of us who follow Christ. Our Christian conscience must force us to act. We must go to public officials — judges and legislators — and demand in the name of our Lord that reforms be made — jails cleaned up, sentencing practices changed — so horrors like these are stopped.

And we must do more. We must expose the ugliness of a society which entertains itself on parlor games like "Capital Punishment," and tolerates real games like those in which the James Pangburns die. We *must* do this — and then lovingly show that there is a better way.

September 1981

Chapter Eighteen

"But, Lord..."

There is an old saying that man's extremity is God's opportunity. And although our nation's current budget crisis is a choice example of that adage, there are some churchmen in New York who certainly missed their cue to respond.

A recent survey revealed that an estimated 36,000 homeless men and women have been wandering New York's streets at night. The city's maximum shelter capacity is just more than 3,500 and the budget is already overloaded, so Mayor Koch appealed to the city's religious leaders for help. If each of New York's 3,500 places of worship would care for just ten homeless people, a desperate human problem would be quickly solved, without huge government expense.

The churches' reactions were not quite what the mayor had hoped for. According to the *New York Times*, some religious leaders were miffed at first learning of the plan through the newspapers. The director of the New York City Council of Churches said: "The mayor has never mentioned this to me. He has not called, and nobody from his office called to apprise me of this."

A spokesman for the Roman Catholic Archdiocese sidestepped in a different way: "It is a very complex situation and the remedy will be complex," as did a representative of the Board of Rabbis: "… there are problems of implementation in many churches and synagogues. During the winter, many turn off their heat at night."

According to the *Times*, the consensus was that the religious leaders needed time to evaluate the proposal. I wonder how it will sound on that day, promised in Matthew 25, when our Lord says, "I was a stranger and you did not invite me in," and the religious leaders respond, "But, Lord, You didn't give us time to study the proposal."

So when put to the test, the church in New York worried more about protocol and prerogatives than human beings. It was more concerned with heating bills than homeless people huddled against its doors to escape subzero winds.

Those homeless in New York are a painful example of a truth we must face. Government cannot provide all of the answers; our country can no longer afford annual spending binges which only end in bloated budgets and double digit inflation. That is immoral, just as if the government were to stick its greedy paw into everyone's savings accounts or pensions, dipping out a hefty 10 percent to feed its insatiable appetite.

But to correct our staggering deficit is a big job, requiring big cuts. So the budget axe is falling — on grants, welfare and aid programs — and tragically, it's the poor who are getting it in the neck.

That's the dilemma. When government cuts back, as many, myself included, believe it should, the poor who have grown dependent on its programs are left stranded. To turn away from their needs is just as immoral as rapacious inflation. Christians should be especially sensitive to this, for Scripture clearly commands us to share God's special concern for the needy.

So the budget crunch can be either an insoluble crisis, like in New York — or a tremendous opportunity. These times present an historic challenge for the church to do its biblical duty, to step in and take up the burdens of the needy which we have too easily passed off to big government. But if we simply nod to that truth without doing anything about it, we are hypocrites. So, the homeless in New York may represent a tough question: do we really mean what we preach and profess?

The problem in New York, I believe, is that church bureaucracies have become just as complacent as government bureaucracies, so wrapped up in writing pious statements of faith and issuing press releases that they have forgotten their reason for existence: to proclaim the Good News and obey the clear commands of our Lord. But I cannot believe that those quoted in the *Times* are representative of the vast majority of concerned pastors and caring laity across this country.

We dare not fail to seize our opportunity. To jump into these areas of need and meet people's crying concerns is a bold leap of faith. It may upset our comfortable lifestyle. But that is what being Christian is all about.

We can do it if we will. Consider our Atlanta Community Service Project, in which we took six convicts out of prison to winterize two widows' homes, and the Agape House ministry. These are tremendous examples of needs being met by a church which is faithful to its biblical call. They prove the job can be done — without red tape, using not a penny of government money.

What an opportunity it is for evangelism! When those in need see that the church genuinely cares for them, they will listen to our message.

That challenge ought to cause us to spill out of our church offices, get up out of our pews, and go into the places of human need and respond as Christ commands. If it does, government austerity may not be such a bad thing after all.

March 1982

Chapter Nineteen

The Contest for Men's Hearts and Minds

We who live in the twentieth-century technocracy, the age of supercomputers and vast bureaucracies, need to be reminded of what a renowned sociologist wrote a century ago: History is but "the visible effects of invisible changes in human thought."

The truth of those words hit home as I watched the extraordinary television coverage of Pope John Paul's visit to Poland. What an incredible sight: a million people gathered for mass in the center of Warsaw, surrounded by Soviet divisions, yet praying and chanting together as one. As the camera panned the vast throng, it caught what was for me an unforgettable scene: millions of arms raised together in the Solidarity salute!

Solidarity is more than a movement for workers' rights; it is a spiritual expression deeply rooted in the church. I could not help but think of Stalin's famous quip when an advisor warned him of church opposition: "The Pope? Ha! How many divisions does *he* have?" What would Stalin say today?

The courage and faith of the Polish people demonstrate once

again that totalitarian muscle cannot stamp out a peoples' vision, that spiritual forces shape history far more than mighty armies. Yes, it is the "invisible changes in human thought" which determine our destiny.

This central truth of history should remind us of our duty to bring the Christian message into the marketplace of ideas. How well we permeate our national consciousness with Christian truth will determine the values our culture lives by.

How are we faring in this crucial struggle? Consider some recent indicators:

A 1979 *Christianity Today* survey revealed that only 26 percent of the general public (and only 43 percent of evangelicals) believe Jesus Christ to be fully God and fully man.

In a recent Gallup survey 81 percent considered themselves Christians, but only 42 percent knew Jesus delivered the Sermon on the Mount — and only 46 percent were able to name the four Gospels.

Other Gallup polls reveal that between 1963 and 1982 the percentage of Americans who believed the Bible infallible dropped from 65 percent to 37 percent.

When 1,382 people were asked what book had most influenced their lives fifteen cited the Bible — barely more than 1 percent!

No wonder there is moral rot — sexual permissiveness and perversion, breakup of the family, soaring crime rates. For the knowledge of God, the foundation of any country's Christian consensus, is collapsing; Christian values are in retreat across the landscape of American life.

Why?

First, it is obvious that we Christians are biblically illiterate, failing miserably to educate ourselves and defend our beliefs to others. (This is a chief reason I wrote *Loving God* — to challenge the believer to understand and take his faith seriously.)

Second, equally obvious, is that the Christian worldview has been undermined by a fierce frontal assault for the past twenty-five years. The judiciary has interpreted freedom of religion to mean freedom *from* religion, striking down Christmas carols and voluntary prayer on public property. Infanticide, or abortion-on-demand, has been repeatedly sanctioned by our highest court. Films and network TV feed viewers a steady diet of violence and increasingly explicit eroticism.

But, startling as it may sound, these attacks are not really what alarm me. Of course they are grave — but also obvious. And there is something we can do about each one, from fighting for a constitutional amendment to protect the unborn to turning off the tube and boycotting products of companies sponsoring trash.

No, what concerns me more than the frontal assault is a more subtle attack — the insidious way Christian ideas are subtly altered by an interpretation here, a nuance there. In the media age the way a reporter simply phrases an issue — often unconsciously — can determine the mindset of millions.

Just one personal example. In thousands of interviews in the past ten years, I have invariably described my conversion as "accepting Jesus Christ." Reporters, equally invariably, translate those deliberate words into "religious experience" or "conversion to Christianity" or sometimes "born again," since that term has been so secularized as to be harmless. Christianity? Fine, it preaches peace. But talk about a risen Lord, the Christ who lives today, and you'll find yourself subtly censored.

A small thing, you say. Maybe. But the cumulative effect of thousands of such news columns over the years is to blunt the sharp edge of the gospel truth, and reduce the living God, Jesus Christ, to merely an "ism," just another cult in American society. This is but one example of what's happening to us.

We must act. For the hard truth is that we Christians are losing the mortal struggle for the hearts and minds of our neighbors. And our most grievous wounds are being inflicted by an invisible enemy.

October 1983

Chapter Twenty

The Contest for Men's Hearts and Minds—Part II

The evidence is overwhelming. We Christians are losing the struggle for the hearts and minds of our neighbors. Christian values, historically the moral foundation of American life, are crumbling.

How can this be so in a nation where 81 percent of the people profess to be Christians?

In the battle for the values our culture lives by, the weapons are often words. Take *gay* for example: a word connoting happiness is misused to mask perversion.

Or consider how abortionists are described as being for "free choice" (that's a good word), they are "progressive" (anything new is better) and are supported by "enlightened" interests. Anti-abortion groups, on the other hand, are against free choice, and therefore "regressive" and "bigoted."

Perhaps you've noticed how the Christian viewpoint is often labeled as "extreme fundamentalism" or coupled with inflammatory adjectives. The December 1981 court challenge to the Arkansas statute allowing creationism to be taught as an alternative to evolution offers a vivid illustration. Consider how *The Washington Post* described the parties involved:

"The ACLU and the New York firm of Skadden Arps attacked the Arkansas law with a powerful case. Their brief is so good that there is talk of publishing it. Their witnesses gave brilliant little summaries of several fields of science, history and religious philosophy." Such was the "enlightened" plaintiff.

The creationist witnesses, however, were "impassioned believers, rebellious educators and scientific oddities. All but one of the creation scientists came from obscure colleges or Bible schools. The one who didn't, said he believed diseases dropped from space, that evolution caused Nazism, and that insects may be more intelligent than humans but are hiding their abilities." It goes on.

The point is simple. If you were an uninformed reader, who would you believe—the firm of Skadden Arps with its brilliant summaries, or the backwoods weirdos from no-name colleges? One can only conclude that in Arkansas in December of 1981, to question evolutionary theory—that is, to be Christian—was to be stupid.

Editorial decisions can have far-reaching implications. One major American daily, for example, never uses the word *Christ* when speaking of Jesus. To do so, its editors believe, would be to make an editorial judgment.

Similarly, when Francis Schaeffer asked PBS to air his *How Should We Then Live?*, a presentation of history, creation and the universe from the Judeo-Christian perspective, he was turned down cold—"too religious."

But the same PBS regularly airs "Cosmos," feeding the viewer a steady diet of "The cosmos is all that is or ever will be." That is as close to a definitive catechism of secular humanism as one can find.

So the secular world gets prime-time coverage while the

Christian world is exiled to its own programming. It's good to have our programs, of course. But by compartmentalizing us, the media effectively refuses to dignify the Christian view as a respectable intellectual alternative in the marketplace of ideas.

These kinds of things often cause us to believe there is a deliberate media conspiracy to destroy the Christian view. But in fact I don't think it is deliberate; it is something much worse — the reflection of the natural, unconscious attitude of the secular observer.

Secular reporters, only 8 percent of whom regularly attend church, understandably cannot discern the significance of spiritual matters. In all the voluminous coverage of Filipino activist Benigno Aquino's assassination, for example, I could find only one or two mentions of his Christian commitment.

But the fact is, it was Aquino's dramatic conversion to Christ which led him to return to the Philippines to "fight hatred with greater Christian love." By failing to see that spiritual truth, the media missed the story altogether.

So a word inserted here, a story ignored there, an interpretation and a nuance at a time, the secular view inexorably gains ground. And what astounds me is that we yell about the blatant eroticism and violence on television — as we should — yet virtually ignore the more insidious ways the media is seizing the mind of our culture.

Have we forgotten that moral confusion is the enemy's favorite weapon? We Christians are called to be discerning — and, while there is yet time to take our stand, we must expose the false values being so insistently perpetrated. We must urgently join in the battle for men's hearts and minds.

Doing so will impose radical demands on the followers of Christ. But we dare not fail — for as people think, so will they act.

November 1983

Chapter Twenty-one

The Contest for Men's Hearts and Minds — Part III

During a recent radio interview I came face to face with the way the secular media — often subtly, sometimes unconsciously — blocks the Christian message from the mainstream of American thought. This time, however, it was not so subtle.

Just before air time, the interviewer leaned across the microphone. "Mr. Colson," she said, "we'll talk today only about prisons; it's against station policy to mention God on the air."

The mike's red light flashed. The interviewer asked about prisons; I talked about the Christ who sends me there. When she objected to my answers, I could only remind her — politely, I hope — that the same First Amendment freedom of press protects my freedom of religion.

I'm not sure the interviewer would agree, but I welcomed the confrontation. It brought into sharp focus the central issue of the day — *what are the values by which we as a people shall live?*

If, as I've argued in this book, we Christians are losing the struggle for those values, then it's time to get off the fence, into the fray, and engage the secular world in head-to-head battle.

What does that really demand of us?

First, we must discern the false values of our culture. Tragically, the church has become so comfortable with the culture it can no longer see the bankruptcy of its egocentric, materialistic ways. Indeed, much Christian literature and preaching is but a religious adaptation of self-indulgent secular standards. But the "what's in it for me," "God will put a chicken in every pot" message mocks the hard-edged truth of the gospel. It is nothing less than heresy.

Second, we must study and know the holy, infallible Word of God and the great theological truths of our faith. Surveys reveal an abysmal biblical ignorance in the American church. No wonder we are losing the real conflict of our age. Without a solid biblical foundation, we are not only unable to defend our faith, but are easy prey for the lures of hedonism and cheap grace.

We need to be in the Word. And instead of puffy testimonies, all with the same happy endings, we need to dig into the classics, from Augustine and Spurgeon to C. S. Lewis and Schaeffer.

Third, we must "crown Him Lord of all," as the great hymn proclaims. The *New York Times* asked the founder of McDonald's what he believed in. "God, my family, and McDonald's hamburgers," he replied, but then added, "and when I get to the office I reverse the order."

His apparently facetious comment masks an ironic truth: for many Christians, God has first priority — on Sunday mornings — but life goes on as usual the rest of the week. Our religious experience is considered private, affecting inner feelings perhaps, but not outward actions.

But being Christian is more than mouthing pious hymns or believing in a vague deity. To follow the Christ of the Scriptures inevitably — and radically — alters one's opinions and values on everything from lifestyle, to the dignity of life, to justice, to art, to intellectual perceptions. It involves the totality of our lives — and only as we grasp that truth and make Chirst Lord of all can we ever hope to make an impact on the totality of our culture.

Fourth, we must take the church to the people. Too often we sit in church as spectators, waiting for the needy multitudes to come watch the show with us. But for those in need — spiritually and physically — a fat, lethargic church preoccupied with its own entertainment holds no appeal.

Our challenge is to get out of our cozy pews and take the gospel to those outside. Jesus didn't set up counseling hours in the Temple; He went into the homes of the most notorious sinners, to the places where the lame, the beggars, the needy could be found.

And when we follow Jesus' lead, the world suddenly pays attention. For example, the media seldom report on one of our church services, but reporters invariably cover our community service projects, in which Christian inmates' weatherize the homes of needy families. Agape House, the home for inmates' families started by PF volunteers, received White House recognition; our reform legislation based on biblical principles has gained national attention as well.

When the world can *see* that Christians care about their neighbors, they also *see* the relevance of the gospel to meet human need. That's wrestling for the hearts and minds of the secular world — *on their turf.*

And finally, we must invade the secular marketplace. Our best writers shouldn't all compete for spots with *Christianity Today* or CBN, for example, but should infiltrate the newsrooms of the *New York Times* and CBS. Christian scholars should debate their secular counterparts and shatter the myth that Christian faith is intellectually inferior. Christian business people need to apply biblical principles to everyday office decisions.

An eminent British scholar argues that America is in a turning point between a Christian and post-Christian culture. I agree. Can we yet prevail in the great ideological transition of this century? The answer lies in whether the church has the courage to boldly take its stand and demonstrate the truths of the gospel of Christ.

Do we?

December 1983

Chapter Twenty-two

Law and Order and Romans 7

Just as the swallow's song heralds the arrival of spring, so the melodious chorus of political rhetoric tells us when election season is at hand.

And it's amazing how, season after season, the song remains the same. *Newsweek* reported last month that Reagan strategists are preparing to make get-tough-on-crime their key October 1984 campaign stance. No surprise. In 1970 I helped run the first off-year campaign of Nixon's Presidency; the polls told us law and order was the juiciest issue, so we rode it like we were campaigning for county sheriff.

But tough talk isn't exclusive to one party. A Democratic gubernatorial hopeful in Georgia campaigned this summer with a genuine electric chair in the back of his pickup truck, promising to plug it in the moment he took office.

Recently I watched a primary debate between five congressional candidates, each outswaggering the others with the tough laws — including mandatory sentencing — they'd pass in Washington to "stop crime." All are intelligent men who know full well that law enforcement is primarily a local responsibility, not Washington's.

Ironically, the U.S. Justice Department had released a study only a few days earlier showing that though mandatory sentencing laws fill up the prisons — at great cost — they do not cut down on crime. Paradoxically, they may even increase it. When New York passed a mandatory life sentence for drug offenders several years ago, drug offenses continued to sky-rocket (as did the prison population). The legislature had to repeal the law.

But no matter. Tough talk gets votes, so candidates talk tough.

The truth is, if stiffer sentences stopped crime, we shouldn't have any crime at all. Consider that the average federal sentence in the U.S. increased from 16.5 months in 1945 to 55 months in 1982 — a nearly 400 percent jump. The crime rate, however, rose correspondingly.

Our country imprisons more people per capita than any other nation except the Soviet Union and South Africa; yet we have the highest crime rate in the world. If that's law and order, spare us any more.

Baffling? Yes, but nothing new. Eighteenth-century British officials tried to cut crime by promoting large crowds to witness the hanging of pickpockets. There was a problem, however. Other thieves had a field day stealing the wallets of those gathered to watch the execution of their fellow pickpockets.

The paradox makes no sense to the secular mind — but the Christian should understand. For where is the anguish of the human soul more poignantly expressed than in Paul's letter to the Romans. "The good that I wish, I do not do; but I practice the very evil that I do not wish." He never wanted to covet, Paul explains in Chapter 7, until the law said "thou shalt not covet." Then he found himself filled with covetousness of every kind.

Why? The sin within us uses the law itself to produce the very offense the law is intended to prevent. But in the next chapter the apostle answers the dilemma: though the law alone could not restrain sin, through Christ we are set free, rescued from the sin which controls us.

In a country where fifty million people claim to be born again, it is astonishing that voters are so blind to this fundamental spiritual truth. That's why politicians get away with playing on public fear every two years, and why we waste billions of dollars applying wrong solutions to the dangerous problem of crime in America.

This is not to suggest that we dispense with the law. It is the first duty of government to restrain sin; punishment is essential to maintain justice. The individual must be held accountable for his actions, and it is the law which represents the standard of accountability. And we *do* need prisons to confine offenders who pose a danger to society (less than half of those we now imprison).

But passing tougher laws and building more prisons isn't going to solve the crime problem. The delusion which vote-hungry politicians perpetrate — that crime can be cured by simple panaceas — is dangerous. It diverts us from the real issue and makes the problem worse.

The only way to combat the demogoguery which so inflames public passions every two years is for Christians to work for laws which apply biblical standards to criminal justice issues. Though the Bible does not prescribe prison as punishment, restitution is called for often, beginning in Exodus 21. And most important we must clearly discern the truth about the nature of man; Romans 7 and 8 is a fine place to begin.

There are some hopeful signs. A few months ago Congressman Dan Coates (R-Indiana), elected two years ago on a so-called "law and order" platform, announced he had changed his views and no longer favors sending nonviolent criminals to prison. A committed Christian, Mr. Coates announced support for restitution, the biblical answer. Predictably, his statements initially set off a ruckus in his district. However, as voters thought through the issue, they began to support his stand.

Of course, there is political risk. But there is often a difference between what is politically expedient and what is biblically sound. And as Christians in government as well as lay people demonstrate this kind of courage, the myths which have so skewed our criminal justice policies will be shattered — and none too soon.

October 1982

Chapter Twenty-three

Human Life: Dignity or Dust?

Not long ago, two Los Angeles doctors stood accused of murder. During a routine operation, Clarence Herbert, fifty-five, slipped into a coma. His condition was diagnosed irreversible; Herbert's family asked that he be removed from life support systems. The physicians first disconnected Herbert's respirator; when he stubbornly refused to expire, they stopped intravenous feeding. Nine days later, Clarence Herbert finally wasted away, cells starved, body tissues shriveled.

One network anchorman commented, "The question of *when* to pull the plug may be about to get a very thorough hearing in a Los Angeles courtroom."

A municipal judge — incredibly, in my mind — dismissed the case. But the issue, unlike the patient, is far from dead.

How subtly semantics can shape a nation's moral agenda! The question now is *when*, not *if*, doctors have a right to kill their patient. And I suspect the anchorman's choice of words was unconscious, merely reflecting the unchallenged worldview of our day. But they brought to mind a scene from what I was reading at the moment — Solzhenitsyn's *Cancer Ward.*

A patient in a Soviet hospital, helping a nurse sort patients' records, notes how few are terminal cases: "I see they don't allow them to die here; they manage to discharge them in time."

The nurse nods. "If it is obvious a patient is beyond help and there is nothing left for him but to live out a few last weeks or months, why should he take up a bed? There is a waiting list for beds."

So those beyond cure are let out to die. For not only is bed space scarce, but a doctor in a Soviet state-run hospital is like any other bureaucrat — too many deaths on his ward ruin the neat statistics his superiors review.

Ironically, during the same years portrayed so bleakly in *Cancer Ward,* a young nun was beginning her ministry of mercy in Calcutta. Mother Teresa discovered a woman dying in a trash pile; no hospital would admit her. The young nun held her as she died, then persuaded government officials to give her space in an old Hindu temple to set up a hospice. And since 1954 countless destitutes have been picked up off the streets, bathed, their sores dressed, so, as Mother Teresa says, "through God, they could die with a smile on their face."

Of course, the difference between Soviet doctors casting out the dying, and Mother Teresa gathering them in, is far more fundamental than the contrasts between totalitarianism and democracy. The real issue, the same one raised by the Los Angeles trial, is a question of *how we view human life*.

If life results from a chance collision of atoms, man is no more than dust returning to dust, with no value beyond his contributions to that element political philosophers call the "common good." And if that's all there is, then we can at least call the Soviet system efficient, for it gets rid of the least useful and saves the most productive.

But the gospel, as Mother Teresa demonstrates, reverses

that dehumanizing view. Man is created by a sovereign God, in His image, so life is sacred.

The question of whether we view life in this way is erupting everywhere. It has been at the heart of two decades of debate over abortion; more subtly, but just as surely, it is involved in such issues as the controversy over nuclear weapons, or the renewed demand for capital punishment.

And it is central to today's emerging medical dilemmas as well. I watched a panel of doctors on "Good Morning America" discuss various techniques for "rationing" medical services which will become increasingly scarce as new scientific break-throughs extend life. One doctor suggested we let economic forces work — those who can afford treatment live, those who can't die. Another physician proposed random selection, or perhaps the establishment of some government agency — which would, of course, lead to ultimate tyranny. No one even raised the moral question.

But the implications here go beyond even these crucial questions, challenging the philosophical foundations upon which our political structures stand. Our nation's very constructs of justice and freedom depend on whether we view life as sacred or not.

For if the individual is without inalienable, God-given dignity, then why treat him justly? And what is justice, anyway? Simply the "common good"?

Gestapo officer Klaus Barbie illustrates the ultimate consequences of this view. "Exterminating the Jews," he says, "was simply the way Hitler did away with unemployment." What a monstrous statement! Yet if some supposed good of the whole at any given moment is more important than one person's dignity, or life, then Barbie's perspective becomes horribly logical. Justice, without an ultimate standard, can only be a matter of expediency.

The L.A. case — and the media response — are but scenes in the great moral drama which will certainly dominate the rest of this century. For as Francis Schaeffer warns us in his masterful book *A Christian Manifesto*, the Christian consensus — which has for centuries sustained the innate dignity of human life — is rapidly being vanquished by a wholly secular mindset.

And perhaps the greatest danger of all is that when the secular world chooses the words and defines the issues, we may never even know about the battle until the war is over.

April 1983

Chapter Twenty-four

Struggling for Men's Hearts

"Mr. Colson, I must talk with you!" An Oriental man with penetrating eyes excitedly grasped my arm as I boarded the crowded jetliner. To avoid commotion in the aisle, I suggested that he sit in the empty seat next to mine.

"My name is Benigno Acquino," he began. "I was in prison seven years and seven months, much of it in solitary confinement." He paused. "I can't believe I am meeting you. I wanted to die in prison until I read your book."

As he recounted his amazing story I remembered where I'd heard his name. Acquino, son of a former Philippine President, was a young, articulate senator and popular opposition leader to President Marcos. When martial law was declared in 1972, Acquino, along with other political dissidents, was thrown into prison.

"The guards used to let the dogs eat half my dinner and then give me what was left," Acquino told me. "I hated everyone. Then my mother sent me your book. Nothing ever touched my heart until *Born Again*."

One night Acquino knelt in his cell and gave his life to Jesus Christ. His viewpoints, his life, his heart all changed. He continued to oppose Marcos, but without his former bitterness and hate. He and his supporters rejected the Marxist teaching they had begun to embrace in the oppression of prison. Then in 1980 he was suddenly freed to come to the U.S. for a triple bypass operation.

"One day I will be back in the Philippines," he told me. The warmth of his smile told me that his heart had never left. "I will either be back in government — or I will be back in prison. Either way, we'll start Prison Fellowship. I promised the Lord that when I walked out of prison."

I thought of Acquino the other day when I received a letter telling me, "The crime problem is so great in America — why are you wasting your time overseas?"

My correspondent is right: the crime problem is horrendous in the United States. But several reasons draw us to minister overseas. The first two are rather obvious. First, the gospel is the hope of *all* people. Jesus calls us to be part of a Holy Nation, one people drawn from all lands joined in a new covenant. And we know that revivals have historically not been confined to one nation. For example, the great lay prayer awakening in the mid-nineteenth century began in Canada, spread to New York City, then leaped across the Atlantic and ultimately impacted the entire English-speaking world.

But Acquino's experience suggests a third less obvious but perhaps even more profound reason for reaching out to foreign prisoners.

In America, we are accustomed to thinking of prisons as filled with "ordinary" lawbreakers — thieves, murderers, maybe embezzlers. But overseas, prisons are also populated by another breed: past and future political leaders. Following a coup, for example, the government leaders who are not executed are cast into prison. Or when political agitators threaten an established regime, as in Acquino's case, they are often silenced by being shut away in prison.

So, foreign prisons are often training grounds for future political leaders. There are many examples. The late President Sadat, whose political and spiritual convictions were shaped in a British prison, described that experience as his most crucial preparation for a world leadership role. Prime Minister Menachem Begin likewise spent time in prison, as did Indira Gandhi, Francois Mitterand, Helmut Schmidt, to name just a few from the current and recent panorama of world leaders. Alexander Solzhenitsyn's powerfully prophetic writings were shaped by his ten years in a Soviet gulag, for it was in prison that he was converted to Jesus Christ.

Like Acquino, Solzhenitsyn is a happier example of the incarceration experience. But the views of many tyrannical Third-World leaders were also formed in the oppression of prison. It was there that they became dangerous revolutionaries.

The Marxists are right when they assert that their struggle is for the hearts and minds of people. They understand that the most powerful human desire in disadvantaged nations is to be free from oppression. Exploiting that desire for freedom, they give an appealing but false label to their "liberation" movement.

And where better to shape their "liberation" leaders than in the dark and angry dungeons of these countries?

Prisons, as Acquino reminds us, can be the battleground for a nation's future. Tomorrow's political leader may be today's political prisoner — and how he or she influences their nation will be determined by that prison experience. What might have happened to the politics of the Western Hemisphere if twenty-five years ago two exiles named Fidel Castro and Che Guevara had been introduced to Christ and consequently chosen to follow the Prince of Peace rather than the Prince of Death? Or what of the staggering ramifications for world history if Adolf Hitler had been led to Christ during his prison term?

This suggests one reason why it is so crucial for the church to work today among the disfranchised and the oppressed of foreign nations; obviously that applies to their prisons. We do not spread an opiate to keep them happy, as the Marxists accuse us, but instead give them the only genuine vision that can liberate man, the good news about the greatest Revolutionary for human freedom who ever lived.

When we obey Christ's command to minister to prisoners, we do not know whose lives we will touch, whether we are in the U.S. or abroad. But there are hundreds of Benigno Acquinos, tomorrow's political leaders, in hate-filled prisons around the world. Introducing them to the gospel of Jesus Christ could be the act that will, through their lives, influence the lives of thousands.

Indeed, prisoners everywhere need to hear the message of the true Liberator, the One who conquered human oppression by becoming oppressed Himself.

April 1982

Chapter Twenty-five

Charity and Freedom

While rereading an essay by Georgi Vins, the Russian pastor imprisoned eight years in Siberia, I was struck by a chilling thought: what Soviet tyranny has failed to do through persecution, we American Christians may unwittingly do to ourselves through indifference. Let me explain.

Lenin and his disciples knew if their Marxist dream was to succeed, they would have to rout out all religious beliefs from their society. Communism is a jealous mistress which tolerates no competing affections. So, after disposing of their immediate enemies, the Soviets turned to their greatest foe: the church.

Most in the West are aware of the consequent persecution of Christians and restrictions on worship. But few realize how deadly has been the assault against the church's social activities. The 1928 legislation controlling "religious cults" expressly forbids the church to collect funds for the poor, to feed the hungry or aid the old and infirm. Church-sponsored education is also outlawed.

It's not hard to see why the Communists viewed the demonstration of Christian compassion as a formidable threat. After all, individual involvement — people helping people — undermines the all-powerful pretenses of a central government. So totalitarian leaders have always repressed individuality, as was made painfully clear when the Polish government ruthlessly abolished the Solidarity movement.

It is in the sinful nature of man — all men, by the way, not just the Stalins and Hitlers — to hunger for power. Since that appetite is insatiable, it is axiomatic that government without restraint inevitably leads to totalitarianism.

Our country's founding fathers understood that truth and wisely constructed a system of checks and balances to prevent excessive concentration of power. They also saw the corollary need for volunteer involvement to meet public need. De Tocqueville wrote that the American experiment in democracy depended on volunteer efforts to protect the individual against the natural tendency of government to grow ever more powerful.

The American church must be reawakened to this truth. In the last half-century, government has mushroomed, its growth accelerated by the incredible computer and communications technology of these times. Coupled with this, polls and social analysts tell us Americans are becoming increasingly insensitive and isolated, absorbed only with self.

Against that backdrop, it is ironic that one of the strongest calls for volunteerism comes from the chief executive of the power-hungry central government. But President Reagan well understands, as did our nation's founders, how crucial individual involvement is to personal liberty.

To add to the irony, the church, which should be the first to respond, seems to be resisting. At a recent White House meeting for religious leaders, Mr. Reagan made an impassioned plea for the religious community to take a greater role in meeting human needs. Though many of us applauded him, some church leaders argued that the government has no right to shrug its responsibilities off onto the church.

We can only imagine how Russian Christians, for fifty years denied the freedom to carry out biblical mandates, might have reacted to that scene: the head of state urging the church to meet human needs, the church leaders pushing those needs back towards the state. How our persecuted brothers and sisters would cherish our freedom to serve!

If we lose our freedom in this country, it won't be because of heavy-handed laws like the Soviet statute of 1928. It will be because an apathetic church has grown sluggish and uncaring, its very indifference fueling the steady growth of government — to the eventual loss of liberty.

This is why organizations like Prison Fellowship, working within the church, are so crucial. Sometimes I'm asked why we bother to organize volunteers, help inmate families, work for criminal justice reform. Why we are not content to simply preach the Good News?

What has happened in the Soviet Union should serve as a good answer: for living out the gospel, as well as preaching it, is what makes the Invisible Kingdom visible, against which no tyrant can stand. Perhaps the Soviet rulers understand better than we the power of what the Apostle James called "pure and undefiled religion — to visit orphans and widows in their distress..."

As Christians we are not only commanded to tithe and serve, we are constrained to do so by the love of Christ. We are to care for those "in distress" out of gratitude for what God has done for us.

But Georgi Vins and thousands like him who live today under vicious Soviet persecution remind us of yet another reason for caring. Individual involvement and voluntary ministries are not only an expression of human freedom; they are a vital part of keeping it.

December 1982

Chapter Twenty-six

Moslem Justice in South Carolina

In a rush of year-end headlines appeared one of the most bizarre stories of 1983, the proposed castration of three South Carolina rapists. It was immediately followed, however, by one of the most poignant — Pope John Paul's visit to his would-be assassin in a Rome prison.

This unlikely pair of news accounts provided an ironic commentary on our faith and culture — and some disturbing insights as well.

The first began in an Anderson, South Carolina courtroom. In hopes of receiving a lenient sentence, three young men charged with a brutal rape confessed.

The judge was in no mood for mercy, however. Thirty years was the sentence, he announced, *unless* ... the young men held their breath ... *unless* the defendants submit to castration!

The crack of the judge's gavel sent shock waves across America. Hoards of reporters descended on the sleepy southern town to cover the defendants' agonizing choice. One immediately chose castration, but asked for more time after consulting with his wife. As of this writing, all three are still deliberating.

Politicians, however, wasted no time in fanning the flames. One state representative proposed bills to televise electrocutions, bring back public hangings, and castrate *all* rapists. "Treat them like animals," he thundered, "so the other animals will understand." Supporters produced referendum petitions, signed by thousands.

The concept of corporal punishment is not new, of course. It is common in Moslem countries, where thieves simply have their hands chopped off in public — a practice which we in the "civilized" West have always found revolting.

But this is not Saudi Arabia. It's South Carolina, the buckle of the Bible belt, where most folks go to church and preachers preach Christ crucified. South Carolina proposing mandatory mutilation?

It would be hard to argue a biblical basis. The Old Testament "eye for an eye" was meant as a restraint on revenge. In the New Testament Jesus rebuffed Peter for slicing off the centurion's ear; Paul described the body as the temple of the Holy Spirit. The Scriptures as a whole emphasize the dignity of the individual, created in the image of God.

Castration raises a host of other questions, as well. Doctors have voiced ethical concerns; so who does it? What about the psychological damage? And is the purpose of law punishment or behavior modification? Timely questions for the eighties.

The practical question is whether castration works. The evidence is that it may not destroy the sex drive. Besides, most experts believe rape a crime of violence rather than sexual passion. So does the judge really want to release confessed rapists who may, castrated or not, still attack people? I don't.

But the most disturbing point in this case centers on public reaction. Many people applauded the representative's statement about "animals." So pervasive is the fear of crime we'll do almost anything against those who perpetrate it, pay any price for the illusion of safety.

That's the real danger. For while I doubt that castration will actually become South Carolina law, the passionate reaction reveals the depth of fear and frustration which grips us. And when faced with the choice between liberty and order, fear-ridden people through the years have chosen order. Germans did so in the early thirties — Hitler, remember, enjoyed overwhelming public support for ridding the streets of criminals. (Jewish merchants came next.)

That couldn't happen in America, you say. But the South Carolina case reminds us how much hatred smolders near the surface of the human soul. And individual liberty can survive only as long as those passions are restrained.

There is another way than Moslem justice. We saw it in the remarkable story of Pope John Paul's visit to Rome's Rabbibia Prison on Christmas Day. Millions around the world watched TV coverage of John Paul's meeting with Mehmet Ali Agca, the twenty-five-year-old Turk who only two years earlier had pumped several bullets into the pontiff's stomach.

The white-robed Pope and jean-clad terrorist huddled in Agca's stark cell for twenty minutes, talking in low voices that could not be overheard. When he emerged John Paul explained, "I spoke to a brother whom I have pardoned ... and the Lord gave us the grace to meet each other as men and as brothers."

Agca, of course, is a Moslem; the Moslem world, which knows not of Christ's forgiveness, was stunned. The Turkish press called the Pope's action "shocking."

So while Bible-belt Christians were clamoring for Moslem justice, the bishop of Rome was witnessing Christian love to the Moslem world.

For me, this spine-tingling scene again affirmed how radically different the gospel is from the world's ways. I could only hope my brothers and sisters in South Carolina were watching as well.

For John Paul's visit to that Rome prison was not only the embodiment of the gospel. Coming on the heels of the ugly story from South Carolina, it should cause us to reflect on the lessons of history—and remember that the price of appeasing our passions for revenge may well be the loss of our freedoms.

February 1984

Chapter Twenty-seven

"Soft" on Crime?

M y desk was piled high with letters responding to some recent national articles about our ministry.

A man from New Mexico suggested a way to reduce the prison population: "Put all repeat offenders in the gas chamber." Another wrote, "Let them rot." One woman proposed that all Prison Fellowship staffers be put with all the "other criminals" on a deserted island.

Letters like these reflect growing public frustration over the crime crisis in America. The crime rate is soaring even as more people are being put in prison than ever before. The government's new task force has recommended $2 billion in federal aid for new prisons, yet experts tell us prisons aren't stopping crime. Nothing seems to work, and public patience is wearing thin.

Since one out of three American households will be affected by crime this year, there are increasing numbers of victims who angrily — and rightly — demand justice.

I understand how they feel. Six years ago our home was burglarized. Among the valuables stolen were White House memorabilia, my college ring and sterling silver pieces my grandfather had made. They were irreplaceable. Patty and I were outraged over losing family relics and, even more, over having the privacy of our home invaded. Ironically, I was out of town visiting a prison the day the burglary took place.

Then, just a year ago, a young man snatched my briefcase in the Miami airport while my back was turned. The briefcase could be replaced, but not the hundreds of speech notes that were in it.

Both times I experienced the full fury of unvented anger. Had I been able to catch the young man in the airport, I might have momentarily forsaken my Christian witness and wrestled him to the ground.

This mixture of fear and fury is a natural — and valid — reaction. But though it is understandable, the very emotionalism of the issue is what threatens hope for a rational solution. Already we are being dangerously polarized. So-called law and order advocates see those of us who want reform as "soft" on crime, as being against punishment.

But this is not the issue. Christians, in particular, understand the need for punishment. Ours is a God of justice who exacts punishment for sin. When Adam and Eve disobeyed His first commandment, God pronounced the sentence all mankind lives under to this day. His wrath is swift and sure, as the Israelites learned when they cajoled Aaron into making the idolatrous golden calf, and as Ananias and Sapphira discovered in the early days of the Christian church.

Despite modern psychologists who argue that societal conditions like poverty cause crime, the Judeo-Christian view sees man as responsible for his own moral choices. Throughout the ordinances given to Moses at Mt. Sinai is the consistent theme of individual accountability. Man is held to account under the threat of punishment for the consequences of his actions.

The biblical rationale for government, in fact, is to preserve order and to restrain man from inflicting his sin upon others. The first example of this was God's stationing the angel with the flaming sword in the Garden of Eden to protect the tree of knowledge. So we Christians are commanded in the much discussed verses of Romans 13 to obey and submit to governing authorities. God has ordained that order be maintained. Government, with its power to protect and punish, is His instrument.

The issue, then, is not *whether* society is to punish, but *how* it is to punish.

The hard truth is that prisons aren't working. In most cases they are not redemptive for the individual, nor are they effective for society.

I remember talking one night in prison with a hardened con who had spent nineteen of his thirty-eight years locked up. He was in for a heavy narcotics offense committed in New York state, which at that time drew a mandatory life sentence. "How in the world could you have done it?" I asked.

"Gee, Chuck," he answered, "I was a rod carrier on the World Trade Center building—eighty floors up, getting $18 an hour. One misstep and I was dead. With hash I could make $300,000 a week. One mistake and it was life in prison."

Many are like this man. The immediate profit is so great they are willing to risk prison, even death. That is why I so strongly favor the punishment so frequently prescribed in Scripture — restitution. Taking the profit out of crime will be a far more effective deterrent than prison. In this area, in fact, some laws need to be tightened up so the assets of organized crime members and heavy narcotics dealers can be seized at the time of arrest. That *is* punishment, and it will work.

But what about violent and dangerous criminals, you ask? Restitution won't protect the public. Don't we still need prisons?

Sadly, the answer is yes. Just as society involuntarily quarantines those with communicable diseases, so it must isolate those who are truly dangerous. And, as columnist Bill Buckley has nobly argued, punishing nonviolent criminals outside of prison in community-based programs will make room in our overcrowded prisons for the truly dangerous, and provide for their more effective, humane treatment.

For Christians, the issue should not be "coddling criminals" on the one hand or "law and order" on the other. The issue must be finding the punishment that is redemptive for the individual and effective for society.

Almost certainly, crime will continue to plague America. President Reagan is promising new initiatives, so the debate will go on. But in the midst of the current hysteria, the Christian duty is to steer clear of demagogic stereotypes and hold fast to biblical truth. For as is so often the case with so many secular issues, it is the Bible that will lead us to the answer.

October 1981

Chapter Twenty-eight

"Forgive Us Our Sins..."

Could you forgive the man who murdered your father?

It seems unthinkable, yet as Christians, we know that Christ commands — and promises to enable — us to do precisely that. "Love your enemies," Jesus tells us; and to love another means to wish the very best for him.

For me, though, forgiveness is one of the toughest aspects of Christian living; and fortunately for most of us, we are never put to such a terrible test of faith as loving one who has killed somebody dear to us.

Ad Coors of Denver, Colorado, who recently joined our board, is one Christian who recently faced just such a duty. With him at a Prison Fellowship rally in Colorado Springs recently, I heard Ad talk about his ordeal for the first time. It provides such a powerful evidence of forgiveness, that I've decided to share it here.

On February 9, 1960, Adolph Coors III was kidnapped and held for ransom. Seven months later, his body was found on a remote hillside — he had been shot to death. Adolph Coors IV, then fifteen years old, had lost his best friend.

The Coors case attracted nationwide attention. A suspect, Joseph Corbett, was apprehended, convicted and sentenced to life imprisonment in the Colorado penitentiary.

For years, through service in the Marine Corps and on into adulthood, Ad Coors harbored hatred for the man who had murdered his father. "I would have done anything in my power to have taken him had I met him," Ad recalls.

Then, in 1975, Ad became a Christian. Soon afterwards, he became part of a fellowship group which included a friend, Dale Morris. "Have you ever forgiven that man?" Dale asked Ad one day. Ad thought a moment and replied, "Sure, Dale. In my heart I have."

Dale pressed the question. "I'm not talking about that. I'm asking whether you've ever gone to him and told him you've forgiven him — and asked for his forgiveness that you've hated him for so long . . ."

It was during this same exchange that Ad learned that Dale was regularly visiting the maximum security unit of Canon City Prison — where the man convicted of killing Ad's father was confined. "Come with me when I go down next Wednesday," Dale exhorted his friend.

"That invitation hit me right in the pit of my stomach," Ad remembers. "There have been few tougher decisions in my life." Three weeks later, Ad made his decision. Dale made arrangements for him to visit Joseph Corbett.

The men arrived at the prison only to learn that the convict had refused to see them. "The funny thing," Ad now recounts, "is that I wasn't relieved — I was disappointed." So he left Corbett a Bible and inscribed it as follows: "I'm down here to see you today. I'm very disappointed that I can't. As a Christian, I have been commanded by our Lord and Savior Jesus Christ to ask for your forgiveness. I forgive you for the sins you have committed against our family, and I ask you to forgive me for the hatred I have had in my heart for you."

To those attending our rally, Ad explained that "Hatred is like the barrel of a shotgun that's plugged. Pretty soon it's going to go off in your face. It hurts the hater more than the hated. It hurt me. It ate me alive, and it ate my family alive."

Remarkably, Ad also told the audience that "Tonight I have a love for that man that only Jesus Christ could have put in my heart."

"Sticking a man in prison and expecting him to reform doesn't work," Ad continued. "It can be done only by forgiveness and a tremendous amount of love, and a knowledge of what Jesus Christ has done for us. That is being done in a dramatic way by Prison Fellowship. That is why — and because of my experience — I feel so drawn to this ministry."

His own knowledge of the grace of Christ has prompted Ad to divest himself of all his interest in the Coors' brewery. Instead, he works as an independent investment adviser and has spent much of his time as a volunteer with Prison Fellowship and other Christian endeavors.

Stories like these, unexplainable apart from an active, supernatural God, make me wonder how anyone can question whether Jesus Christ lives.

August 1980

Chapter Twenty-nine

As We Forgive Others

During a TV interview a few years ago, I mentioned that I could not vote. I was living in Virginia, which denies ex-convicts living voting rights — as well as a host of other civil liberties — for life.

A few days later an old friend called from Richmond. It seems several state officials who had seen the telecast wanted me to know that though Virginia's constitution prohibited the legislature from restoring felons' civil rights, it allowed the governor to act on individual applications. If I would write a letter to the governor, who knew me, he could restore my right to vote.

I was elated as I told Patty that evening. "Does that apply to all ex-convicts," she asked, "or just to you because you're well-known?" (It's good when we have loving spouses who keep us humble.)

That did it. My decision wasn't especially noble; Patty simply left me no choice. The next day I called my friend, thanked him, and explained I would wait until the law was changed for *all* ex-convicts.

So I was encouraged later when a constitutional amendment setting standards for restoring felons' voting rights was added to the Virginia ballot. Surely it seemed fair. After all, since the women's suffrage campaign earlier this century and the civil rights movement of two decades ago, the right to vote has been assured for all Americans — except the hundreds of thousands, perhaps millions, of ex-convicts in Virginia and twenty other states who remain disenfranchised.

But in one of the 1982 election's little noticed results (ignored by even the local press) the amendment was defeated by nearly two to one — 643,470 against, 384,066 in favor.

I was shocked. It's a tragic injustice that felons in Virginia will continue to be denied their civil rights for life — but what the vote says about us as a people is even more tragic.

Virginia is a Bible belt state grounded in religious tradition; its pastors must certainly preach about forgiveness from time to time. "Forgive us our debts *as* we have forgiven our debtors," more than 40 percent of the population prays regularly in churches across the state. Yet many of those who chant the Lord's Prayer so faithfully are the same folks who support a justice system which punishes offenders for decades after they leave prison — an explicit refusal of forgiveness.

Of course, true forgiveness does not imply a soft view of punishment. To the contrary — the God of Israel demands that individuals be held accountable. Punishment is essential to justice. Yet Old Testament discipline for wrongdoing was swift, appropriate to the crime and final — not meted out by slow degrees for the remainder of the offender's life. Leviticus 6, for example, spells out the punishment for robbery, extortion and perjury; the offender was to pay back his victim in full plus one fifth more, then bring a guilt offering to the priest. Once these were carried out, the Lord's words are direct: " ... then he shall be forgiven for any one of the things which he may have done to incur guilt."

Remember too that Joshua was commanded to establish cities of refuge in the Promised Land to which those who had committed manslaughter might flee and be spared from revenge. God was concerned then — as now — with protecting felons from society's tendency to inflict its vengeful passions on those it judges.

It's not that denying rights is always wrong. After all, denying a murderer the right to own a gun or a drunk driver the right to drive are reasonable precautions for public safety. Denying felons their right to vote for life, however, is a senseless denigration of their worth and dignity.

Especially when our national standards of felonies are so arbitrary: it is a felony in Florida to kill another person's animal, but a misdemeanor to deprive a child of food or shelter. In Indiana a man is in prison for the felony of stealing a loaf of bread and a bottle of milk. Marijuana possession is a felony in most states, including Virginia.

A host of individual injustices result from these capricious definitions. Criminal records show the majority of felonies are committed by those under twenty-one. Yet many who straighten out their lives can never escape the dark shadows of their early years. A few years ago a federal statute required commodities brokers to register with a new federal agency. A successful middle-aged businessman, a strong leader in his church and community, did so — only to be forced to resign. A government computer check turned up a criminal conviction in his early twenties. Having paid for his crime twenty-five years ago, he is now paying again.

If offenders are told no matter how hard they work they will be second-class citizens for life, many decide they may as well be what society has already condemned them to be — losers. The FBI says 74 percent of such offenders are rearrested within four years. No wonder — ostensibly free, they are in fact denied true freedom, the chance to regain their rights and dignity.

The great Virginia statesman Thomas Jefferson had a good deal to say about freedom. His eloquent defense of man's "inalienable rights" laid the philosophical cornerstone of our republic — a proud tradition that a majority of Virginians betrayed this past election day.

But perhaps this vote will yet awaken the Christian conscience. The unbiblical injustices in the constitution of Virginia and those of twenty other states should be eliminated. As voters and individual Christians, let us not fail to heed Jesus' words: "If you do not forgive men, then your Father will not forgive your transgressions."

January 1983

Chapter Thirty

Crown Him Lord of Prime Time

I have argued that we Christians — fifty million strong, according to the polls — aren't truly making Christ Lord of all. If we were, the nation wouldn't be in such a moral mess.

Some friends have taken offense. "You can't blame us," one protested. "The major influence in the country today is TV! The networks pump out that garbage — and what can we do?"

Fair point, TV *is* the single most powerful medium of communication; current studies show that the TV set is turned on in U.S. homes an average of seven hours per day! Though some of it is quality programming, much of it simply promotes moral decay. Just look at the soaps (which a lot of impressionable children do): violence, homosexuality, abortions, adultery and avarice are daily fare.

By the end of high school, these malleable young people have seen an average of 350,000 commercials. That is the equivalent of *one and one-half years* of eight-hour workdays — an immense amount of sales hype that saturates young minds in materialistic values.

And TV inevitably influences behavior. After a recent program about a battered wife who burned her husband in bed, a viewer's response was to burn his wife in bed. Just a few weeks ago I read the letter of a twelve-year-old who had sex with his girlfriend — also twelve — because "we saw it on TV and wanted to see what it was like."

Perhaps even most frightening of all, we have become dependent on TV as the "only thing that gives us a sense of commonality as a culture," says Professor George Gerbner of the Annenberg School of Communications. TV, our common bond? A chilling thought.

So what can we do? Certainly we can boycott companies which sponsor trash; we can petition the networks. Mobilizing public pressure is a fair weapon in a free society.

But a recent experience has caused me to wonder whether such efforts miss the point — and let *us* off the hook. I was at a dinner, seated next to the president of one of the three major networks. *A tremendous opportunity*, I thought. I told how millions of Christians were offended by the kind of programming the networks provided.

Knowing TV executives are keenly interested in profit and loss statements, I suggested it would be good business to air wholesome family entertainment. "After all," I said, "there are fifty million born-again Christians out there."

He looked at me quizzically. I assured him that was Gallup's latest figure.

"What you're suggesting, Mr. Colson, is that we run more programs like, say, *Chariots of Fire*?"

"Yes!" I exclaimed, "That's a great movie with a marvelous Christian message."

"Well," he said, "CBS ran it as a prime-time movie just a few months ago. Are you aware of the ratings?"

All at once I knew I was in trouble.

He then explained: That night NBC showed *On Golden Pond*; it was #1 with 25.2 percent of all TV sets in America tuned in. Close behind was *My Mother's Secret Life*, a show about a mother hiding her past as a prostitute. It was #2 with 25.1 percent.

And a distant third — a big money loser — was CBS with *Chariots of Fire* — 11.8 percent. In fact, of the sixty-five shows rated that week, "Dallas" was #1, *Chariots of Fire*, #57.

"So," my companion concluded, "where are your fifty million born-again Christians, Mr. Colson?"

Good question. Where are we?

If even half of Gallup's fifty million born-again Christians had watched the show with the Christian message, *Chariots of Fire* would have topped the ratings. But the disturbing truth, as studies by the secular networks as well as the Christian Broadcasting Network show, is that the viewing habits of Christians are not different than those of non-Christians!

Since TV is a business, it gives its customers — the public — what they want. It is but a mirror image of us. How then can we complain, mount petition campaigns and boycotts when we are watching — along with the rest of the crowd — the very thing we're protesting?

So what does the Lordship of Christ mean in the TV age? First, we need to examine ourselves; values inevitably change as God works in one's life. If we aren't being offended by much of TV (not just the sex and violence, but the intelligence-insulting banality), we need to question whether we are really being "transformed by the renewing of [our] minds." Our discernment as Christians should cause us to turn off offensive programming. It should also make us question whether we are being good stewards of our time. After all, there are some good alternatives to TV. We can read the Bible, explore good Christian writing, spend time with our children, parents, friends.

If we can't turn it off, it may be because TV is addictive. One friend who discovered he was hooked did what any addict must do: abstain. He took the TV out of his house altogether: "If your eye (cathode) offends you, pluck it out." For ten years now my friend and his family have not only survived the TV's loss, but have actually flourished.

When we arrive in heaven and account for the stewardship of our time, will Christ say, "Well done" to, say, one and a half years of TV commercials?

Christ must be Lord of all, yes, even of prime time.

January 1985

Chapter Thirty-one

The Trivialization of Sin

Recently commissioner John Svahn announced that for the first time the Social Security system will be forced to borrow money — $7 billion just for starters. But that would hold things together only until next July. Unless Congress acts quickly, Social Security will be broke.

This was shocking news. But even more alarming was the lack of public reaction. The networks were virtually silent; newspapers in retirement areas gave but a few inches to the story; and a preoccupied Congress adjourned leaving the issue stewing on the back burner.

The U.S. government is promising Americans retirement funds it doesn't have — and can't have under present law! That empty promise is, in plain terms, immoral. If you or I did the same with our own debts we'd be prosecuted for fraud — but the government seems to get away with it.

As disturbing as the lack of public outrage was a statistic buried deep in Svahn's speech. A poll reported that 70 percent of the country does not believe Social Security benefits will exist when they retire.

So not only does the government act unconscionably, but nearly three-quarters of the population condones that immorality by accepting it! Our silence makes us not victims of the corrupt system, but passive participants. We are, in fact, co-conspirators.

And, incredibly, we seem to resist efforts to right the situation. I recently asked a top Republican leader, "Why doesn't the leadership of Congress get together with the President, tell the truth about Social Security, and do whatever it takes to solve the problem?"

He looked at me as if I'd committed public blasphemy and said in shocked tones, "We have a poll showing that one-third of all Republican congressmen would be defeated if we did that!"

So political pressures take top priority. The government perpetuates an empty but pleasant-sounding promise; the people, knowing it is wrong, refuse to hold government accountable.

A *Washington Post*/ABC poll gives further insight. Sixty-four percent of the public believes most congressmen would make campaign promises they had no intention of keeping; 73 percent said the majority of representatives would lie if the truth would hurt them politically. Yet other surveys show most incumbents being reelected.

Those polls, if accurate, tell us the very fabric which holds our free society together is unravelling. People believe that most of their leaders are basically immoral, but accept it. Consequently, the integrity of both government and the people it represents is in shambles.

In Israel the succession of corrupt kings after Solomon brought on the decline and captivity of God's chosen nation. One of their line, Ahab, did "more evil than all who were before." But the people didn't object; 1 Kings records it was "as though it had been a trivial thing for him to walk in the sins of Jeroboam."

Ahab's gross immorality was what the people expected and accepted — so an entire nation considered it trivial to drift after Ahab, flouting God's laws and bowing before Baal. The great prophet Elijah cried out to the Lord, "...the sons of Israel have forsaken Thy covenant!"

Americans today participate in an idolatry all the more insidious because it is less visible. The same root problem infects us that plagued Elijah's day — we trivialize immorality by accepting it as a way of life.

Hope can be found in Scripture. For God responded to Elijah, "I will leave 7,000 in Israel, all the knees that have not bowed to Baal." A remnant of God's people were faithful and did not acquiesce in the sins of their culture. The same can be true in our nation if the Christian's conscience can be awakened.

First, believers must stand for what is right rather than drift with what is wrong. And when we call for biblical standards of righteousness, we'll find we are drawn together in unity. Conservative theologian Francis Schaeffer wrote to me that our only hope is in a radical stance. Liberal Jim Wallis of *Sojourners* uses similar language. Though each man carried different burdens on his heart, they were saying the same thing. We can no longer sit idly by — Christians must, if necessary, defy immoral authority.

Second, we should support men and women of demonstrated integrity. That quality is, I would suggest, far more important than labels of conservative or liberal, Democrat or Republican. There are leaders in government who will do what is right no matter the consequences. And we should express our moral outrage to those who don't.

Social Security is a great place to start. Why not contact your representatives? Serve notice it is time to put all posturing aside. Demand they deal with Social Security before it bankrupts us. Politicians can't resist a wave of true righteous indignation — and that's what our nation so desperately needs.

When we, the people, accept immorality from our government, that's what we get — and we deserve it. But more than that, as the lesson of Israel teaches, we'll get the judgment of God. And we'll deserve that as well.

November 1982

Chapter Thirty-two

The Terrifying Truth: We Are Normal

In the course of research for *Loving God*, I discovered a dearth of contemporary writings on sin. After a long search, however, an unlikely source — Mike Wallace of "60 Minutes" — furnished just what I was looking for.

Since Christians are not accustomed to gleaning theological insights from network TV, I'd better explain.

Introducing a recent story about Nazi Adolf Eichmann, a principal architect of the Holocaust, Wallace posed a central question at the program's outset: "How is it possible ... for a man to act as Eichmann acted? ... Was he a monster? A madman? Or was he perhaps something even more terrifying: was he normal?"

Normal? The executioner of millions of Jews *normal?* Most self-respecting viewers would be outraged at the very thought.

The most startling answer to Wallace's shocking question came in an interview with Yehiel Dinur, a concentration camp survivor who testified against Eichmann at the Nuremburg trials. A film clip from Eichmann's 1961 trial showed Dinur walking into the courtroom, stopping short, seeing Eichmann for the first time since the Nazi had sent him to Auschwitz eighteen years earlier. Dinur began to sob uncontrollably, then fainted, collapsing in a heap on the floor as the presiding judicial officer pounded his gavel for order in the crowded courtroom.

Was Dinur overcome by hatred? Fear? Horrid memories?

No; it was none of these. Rather, as Dinur explained to Wallace, all at once he realized Eichmann was not the godlike army officer who had sent so many to their deaths. This Eichmann was an ordinary man. "I was afraid about myself," said Dinur. " ... I saw that I am capable to do this. *I am ... exactly like he.*"

Wallace's subsequent summation of Dinur's terrible discovery — "Eichmann is in all of us" — is a horrifying statement; but it indeed captures the central truth about man's nature. For as a result of the Fall, *sin is in each of us* — not just the susceptibility to sin, but sin itself.

The 3,500 years of recorded history confirm this truth. Science, evolution and education — which Socrates argued would eliminate sin — have done nothing to alter man's moral nature. Only the gospel of Jesus Christ can change our hearts. But we can't see that truth unless we first see our hearts as they really are.

That being so, why is sin so seldom written or preached about? Dinur's dramatic collapse in the Nuremburg courtroom gives us the clue. For to truly confront evil — the sin within us — is a devastating experience.

If the reality of man's sin was forthrightly preached, it would have the same shattering effect on blissful churchgoers that it had on Dinur. Many would flee their pews never to return. And since church growth is today's supreme standard of spirituality, many pastors steer away from such confrontative subjects; so do authors who want their books bought and read. So do television preachers whose success depends on audience ratings; for viewers confronted with hard truth can simply flick the offending preacher out of their living rooms.

The result is that the message is often watered down to a palatable gospel of positive thinking which will "hold the audience." That's what Nazi victim Dietrich Bonhoeffer called "cheap grace" — that in which "no contrition is required, still less any real desire to be delivered from sin."

But it's the very heart of a Christian conversion to confront one's own sin and thus to desperately desire deliverance from it. And once we've seen our sin, we can only live in gratitude for God's amazing grace. I know this most intimately from personal experience.

During the throes of Watergate, I went to talk with my friend Tom Phillips. I was curious, maybe even a little envious, about the changes in his life. His explanation — that he had "accepted Jesus Christ" — baffled me. I was tired, empty inside, sick of scandal and accusations, but not once did I see myself as having really sinned. Politics was a dirty business, and I was good at it. And what I had done, I rationalized, was no different from the usual political maneuvering. What's more, right and wrong were relative, and my motives were for the good of the country — or so I believed.

But that night when I left Tom's home and sat alone at my car, my own sin — not just dirty politics, but the hatred and pride and evil so deep within me — was thrust before my eyes, forcefully and painfully. For the first time in my life, I felt unclean, and worst of all, I could not escape. In those moments of clarity I found myself driven irresistibly into the arms of the living God.

And in the years since that night, I've grown increasingly aware of my own sinful nature; what is good in me I know beyond all doubt comes only through the righteousness of Jesus Christ. And for that *fact*, my gratitude to God deepens with each passing day, a gratitude that can only be expressed in His service.

Dinur, the Auschwitz survivor, is right — Eichmann is in us, each of us. But until we can face that truth, dreadful as it may be, cheap grace and lukewarm faith — the hallmarks of ungrateful hearts — will continue to abound in a crippled church.

July 1983

Chapter Thirty-three

Into the Looking Glass

Following my testimony before the Delaware legislature on a hotly debated criminal justice reform proposal, one representative cross-examined me closely.

"Okay, Mr. Colson, you make sense," he said. "But what do I tell my constituents when a convict gets out of prison and leads a lot of innocent kids into drugs?"

He then recited an all-too-familiar story: A young man from a broken home gets into trouble, is sent to the state pen, becomes a model prisoner, and is released six months early. But with no family, no job and no one to help him, he is soon back on drugs—and with other kids, back in trouble.

"My phone has been ringing off the hook," the representative continued. "I've never heard folk in our small town so angry. They want this kid locked up forever."

I tried to point out the obvious flaws in the constituents' logic: the young man was going to be released in six months anyway; getting out early didn't change the final outcome. And the basic problem was drugs, for which prisons offer little help. As prison officials agree, prisons do not rehabilitate.

But what is not so obvious is what those irate calls really tell us about ourselves. Sure, people are angry — justifiably so — about crime. But there's more to it.

The constituents' reaction, I believe, illustrates how completely we have been taken in by the political illusion of which Jacques Ellul wrote so masterfully — the widespread notion that every problem must have a government solution.

This dangerous illusion not only inflates government power, it lulls people into feeling they are helpless — even about things in their own backyard.

Just look at the absurdity the illusion created in the Delaware story: here are small-town folk who for years watched a young lad grow up without parents, predictably headed for trouble. Then they become enraged when the state penitentiary, where kids are embittered and often brutalized, cannot cure the result of twenty years of community neglect.

Of course there is nothing new about our tendency to avoid our own responsibility and blame others. Remember Adam's response when God confronted him with his disobedience: "Not me, it was the woman." And Eve in turn responded with a line popularized by Flip Wilson in the seventies: "The devil made me do it."

We Christians have fallen into the same trap. We take refuge from society's decadence in our pious enclaves, and rant and rave about the culture as if it were some distant evil empire.

But we forget so easily that the culture is nothing more than a collection of individuals of which we are a part — and for whom our Lord has given us a special responsibility. He has commanded us to be salt and light in the midst of the world.

In Jesus' day, salt was used not only as flavoring, but more important, as a preservative. Meat could be saved from spoilage only when salt was rubbed in, permeating it.

It is the same with the culture. Made up of sinful people, it will inevitably rot unless Christians permeate its very fiber.

So the painful truth comes back to us: Society's failures are our own responsibility; its values reflect how well—or poorly—we have obeyed our Lord's command to be salt.

Many evangelicals have sought to solve our culture's problems from the top down, by "taking dominion over America." Such rhetoric may make us conspicuous in the news, but for the most part we are also conspicuous by our absence from the day-to-day battles where human problems are most acute.

Happily, there are some encouraging signs. I came across one recently. Jerry Falwell and the Thomas Road Baptist Church, outspoken abortion critics, are not content just to write news releases or hold press conferences. Through their "save a baby" program, they offer a way out to young women in their community who might otherwise believe the lie that abortion is the only "practical" solution. Providing medical help, housing, counseling and an adoption program, these volunteers are making a loving—and Christian—difference in their community. Falwell has helped start hundreds of such centers across the country.

Another practical example can be found in Prison Fellowship's ex-prisoner ministries. Volunteers from churches around the country work with released prisoners providing homes, jobs, and fellowship. These Christians make the difference between ex-prisoners succeeding on the outside or returning to prison.

Yet there is much more to do, and too few people awakened to the need. The beginning of solving problems is to understand that our communities are our responsibility—simply telling off the local politician doesn't let us off the hook.

So, I told that Delaware representative, the next time he receives an angry call he might suggest his constituent take a good look in the mirror. For if we really want to know who's causing the breakdown in our society, we will find more answers in the looking glass than in the state capitol.

September 1984

Chapter Thirty-four

In Search of the Evil Empire

We Americans have a propensity for putting things and people into neat categories. Like in the old movies when all villains wore black waxed mustaches and swirling capes, and all heroes were tall, robust and blond. The "cops and robbers, good guy and bad buy" mentality is as American as apple pie.

And we like to be told how good we are. So every President since Eisenhower has quoted the well-known line attributed to de Tocqueville: "America is great because she is *good*. And if America ever ceases to be *good*, America will cease to be great." It's good politics, a sure-fire applause getter.

But the problem comes when we begin to believe our own press releases, for these pleasant platitudes can pervert our view of the nature of man — dangerously so. President Reagan's controversial speech this spring urging the National Association of Evangelicals to oppose the nuclear freeze movement provides a case in point.

"We know that living in this world means dealing with...the doctrine of sin ... There is sin and evil in the world. And we are enjoined by Scripture and the Lord Jesus to oppose it with all our might," the President proclaimed to the thunderous applause of 1,500 evangelical church leaders. Then Reagan put the issue squarely: the Communists are "the focus of evil in the modern world," and so U.S. military strength is essential to restrain the "aggressive impulses of an evil empire."

Some critics had near apoplexy over the President's speech. It is "illegitimate in the American system ... [to] use sectarian religiosity to sell a political program," shrieked Anthony Lewis of the *New York Times*. "Foul," cried others, that Reagan should mix religion and politics.

Nonsense. There is nothing unusual about politicians using church forums to advance their causes (freeze supporters openly court religious groups). What is more, the nuclear question is a profoundly moral issue, and evangelicals had better face up to it.

No, the difficulty is not in the President urging church people to back a position he keenly believes is in the interest of national security. *The problem is in his theology* — though his appreciative audience didn't seem to mind.

For the Bible tell us that *all* men and women share the same natural disposition. As common heirs of the Fall we *all* are sinners. And we are not sinners because we sin, as theologian R.C. Sproul says, we sin because we are sinners. For the sin is in us.

Yet we in the U.S. persist in believing that humanity (at least the American species) is really innately good, and can eventually be perfected through evolution and education. (Socrates made the same argument — but the history of 2,000 years has done nothing but prove him wrong.) This belief that we can make ourselves better, and are in the process of doing so, is the very essence of humanism. It is also the most subtle and dangerous delusion of our times.

And whichever side of the political spectrum we align ourselves with, this false theology can blind us. On the right, it can breed a dangerous chauvinism, justifying "holy crusades" against "evil empires"; on the left, it often causes us to see no evil in our adversaries, and thus undercuts morally justified deterrent defenses.

In domestic affairs, this blindness to our sin can be equally pernicious. It's one reason our criminal justice system, for example, is in such a shambles. Some liberals believe that since man is really good, when he breaks the law it must be society's fault. Man is not depraved, they say, just deprived — which sounds compassionate but is deadly, destroying all sense of individual accountability.

Some conservatives, on the other hand, believe that the vast majority of people (the good folks, that is) ought to be protected from those flawed few who should be locked up forever. Hence life imprisonment for a nonviolent thief who had stolen $221 worth of merchandise.

We will never find answers to our problems, at home or abroad, until we face the truth about the human condition. Yet our very nature makes us invariably look for evil everywhere except the one place we're sure to find it. And sadly the church all too often fails to preach the convicting truth.

America's blend of civil religion, humanism and comforting platitudes may be good politics — but good politics can make bad theology. Ironically, one of the most discerning voices of our times is a former prisoner of the "evil empire" President Reagan spoke about. Following his conversion to Christ in the Soviet gulag, Alexander Solzhenitsyn wrote, " ... it was disclosed to me that the line separating good and evil passes not through states, nor between classes, nor between parties either — but right through every human heart — through all human hearts."

The evil empire? We needn't search distant continents. The Bible tells us where to look. It is in us.

June 1983

Chapter Thirty-five

"The Punishment of Sin..."

Big headlines recently reported another shocking increase in crime. Violent crimes are up 11 percent, more homicides in Washington, D.C. than in Sweden and Denmark combined.

The experts are baffled, the public demands something be done. But the first question that must be answered is, Why is there so much crime in America? How can this be happening in what purports to be the most civilized society in the world?

Unfortunately, there is no simple answer; understanding human behavior is a complicated business. But two recent well-publicized events, plus a fascinating book I've just read, may provide some insight into an underlying cause.

Consider, as the first example, the Scarsdale Diet doctor murder case. Apparently Dr. Herman Tarnower felt that his wealth and celebrity status freed him from the need to be committed in his relationships. He carried on many affairs with various women, promising to marry them and then when he tired of them, buying them off with money, jewelry, and even the drugs to which his profession gave him easy access.

One of his mistresses was Jean Harris. On the surface Jean Harris seemed to have achieved everything our society has to offer: she was a professional success, headmistress of a posh girl's school near Washington, D.C.; her job gave her entry into an elite capitol social circle, where she was highy regarded as smart, witty and charming, and of course free to carry on with the glamorous diet doctor. What more could she want?

As the lengthy trial revealed in excruciating detail, Jean Harris could and did want a lot more — especially the commitment the doctor wasn't prepared to offer. When he finally tried to discard her, as he had others, for a younger woman, the offers of money and drugs didn't work. Nearly insane with jealousy, grief, pride and drug dependency, Jean Harris ended up shooting the doctor four times. Now, after her protracted courtroom ordeal, she is beginning a long jail term, utterly alone, her career shattered, her lover dead.

Consider next the case of John and Rita Jenrette. While a South Carolina congressman, John Jenrette fell into the net of the FBI's ABSCAM investigation, and was convicted of taking a bribe, defeated for reelection, and now faces a prison sentence. To make matters worse, his wife Rita has filed for divorce, charging him with numerous adulteries, drunken binges and related shenanigans.

Rita Jenrette, however, didn't act much like a wronged woman. Apparently determined to retain the glamorous life to which she became accustomed as a congressional wife, Rita rushed into the kleig lights, to pose for *Playboy*. A generation ago such a performance would have been regarded as shameful except in seamy strip joints, but now in 1981 the international media danced to her tune. Press conferences were packed, fancy luncheons held in her honor in New York's poshest clubs, a fat book contract signed — instant stardom. For weeks she seemed to get more press than the President.

When asked on a TV interview whether she felt any responsibility to her embattered husband, or the constituents they had served, she sighed, managed a coy smile, and said, "I've paid my dues."

When do we ever pay our dues for commitment, once revered as sacred? And we have then made her a genuine celebrity, to the lustful cheers of millions of males and the applause of some feminists who admired her courage.

While watching these tawdy soap operas unfold across my TV screen, I was finishing a gripping book, *The Executioner's Song*. While author Norman Mailer is no model of morality (at last report he is working on his fifth marriage), the book is a masterful retelling of a chilling and important story, the life and death of Gary Gilmore. Despite its frequently vulgar prose, it is must reading for those who deal with prisoners.

Mailer details the months after Gilmore's release from prison, when he was jumping in and out of bed with girls who had been doing the same thing since they were eleven years old. The hedonistic joyride, complete with drugs, six-packs, and eroticism, proved utterly senseless and ended up with two equally senseless killings for which Gilmore was convicted and executed. All the while, Gilmore was obviously seeking to know God, and tragically failing. His empty consolation was to become a media event.

The toll of these three cases has been high: Gilmore's two victims, their killer, and the diet doctor all dead; two other people facing long prison sentences; a marriage destroyed and a wife left in the dubious custody of our society's flesh peddlers. They are very different cases in many ways, but from them emerges a common thread and two lessons, which incidentally tell us more about ourselves than the celebrated principals.

To the eyes of the believer, these cases demonstrate the futility of life without Christ. Mailer's book is, unintentionally I am sure, a powerful Christian witness. For Herman Tarnower, Gary Gilmore, and his two innocent victims, the race is over. For the others, and the rest of us who form their national audience, the lesson is still there for the learning, and the grace of God for the taking.

Second, these cases, and the public response to their popularization, demonstrate once again the truth of what Augustine wrote so long ago: "The punishment of sin is sin." In our society sins are often reported in full detail, then glamourized and finally made highly profitable. Our society continues to reject biblical virtues and to exalt, even reward, sin. Is it really so hard to understand then, why crime, a most visible manifestation of sin, flourishes in our land?

April 1981

Chapter Thirty-six

Can Revival Save America?

*"Mr. Colson, what's wrong in our country? Why can't we
get a revival going that will save America?"*

The questioner — a distinguished looking man, probably in his
early sixties, dressed in a three-piece pinstripe suit — fitted
comfortably into the opulent surroundings of the downtown city
club where I was speaking to twenty-five community leaders. My
topic that morning had been the need for a genuine spiritual
awakening.

I've been asked this same question hundreds of times. Most
often by people like this businessman who fear runaway inflation
and the creeping encroachment of big government. To many of
them "revival" is a magic word. It means having the sort of close
relationship with God which just might offer side benefits as well.
With traditional values and authority caving in, they hope God
can be cajoled by the "revived" into saving our well-heeled lifestyles, protecting our positions and possessions.

Their anxieties reflected by this question are epidemic in our nation today. A glance at best-seller titles makes that clear: *Looking Out for Number One, Crisis Investing, How to Prosper in the Coming Bad Times*, and on and on. It is understandable — and very human — that amid such uncertain times we want to cling to what we have, yearning nostalgically for the "good old days." But while millions of Americans, myself included, pray fervently for revival, we must ask ourselves whether we are asking God to save our society, ourselves, or our souls. Whether we actually know what God demands of us. Whether we really know what revival is. Far from being linked with prosperity or the righting of precarious economies, the great revivals in the history of the church have begun when people have had to submit totally, in ways that seem antithetical (by human and cultural standards) to everything they should have done to survive.

A prime example is England at the time of the Second Great Wesley Awakening. Parliament's vote to support the crusading Christian Parliamentarian Wilberforce and put a stop to slave trade voted directly against their own economic interests as a nation.

There are recent awakenings in nations such as Romania, Argentina and the Soviet Union that have come about under conditions of great human oppression. The key seems to be that only when individuals, whether by will or by force, subordinate their own interests and desires for self-preservation, God can begin to move in a powerful way.

The message here for American Christians is put most powerfully in Alexander Solzhenitsyn's prophetic words written amid unspeakable human suffering in a Soviet prison: "The meaning of earthly existence is not, as we have grown used to thinking, in prosperity, but in the development of the soul" (*Gulag Archipelego II*).

Normally, I avoid a direct answer to this revival question when I think, like I did on this morning, that the questioner is more concerned about his pocketbook than about genuine spiritual awakening. But on this morning, tired from tours of several prisons and a hard night on a lumpy hotel mattress, I responded forthrightly. "The real trouble is that we Christians are not willing to accept the gospel for what it is," I said. "It doesn't tell us how to save anything but our souls.

"You see," I continued, "it's a two-edged sword. Jesus came not only to comfort the afflicted, but to afflict the comfortable. Any hope for revival must begin with genuine repentance, our willingness to give up what we have, and our desire to change."

As I studied the expressions around the table, I realized that idea of giving up what we have — losing our lives for His sake, as Christ tells His disciples to do — is not any more popular today, in our obsessively materialistic society, than it was to the rich young ruler.

Before any awakening can begin, I am convinced that we Christians must come to terms with some hard spiritual truths, just as Solzhenitsyn did in prison. Instead of "using" the gospel to protect what we have, we need to come before our sovereign Master in repentance and surrender.

Revival is God's work; man cannot engineer it. But if we in good conscience ask our sovereign Creator to favor us with a mighty moving of His Spirit, we must obey His clear commands and never distort His gospel for our own self-seeking purposes.

The gospel is good news. But Jesus never said it was easy news. The central truth about the cross is death before life, repentance before reward. Before His gospel can be the good news of redemption, it must be the bad news of the conviction of sin.

June 1981

Chapter Thirty-seven

Can Revival Save America?
Part II

Many remember Mickey Cohen, infamous gangster of the postwar era. One night Cohen attended an evangelistic meeting and seemed interested. Realizing what a dramatic impact his conversion could have on the world, many Christian leaders began visiting him. After one long night session, he was urged to open the door and let Christ in, based on Revelation 3:20. Cohen responded.

But as the months passed, people saw no change in his life of crime. When confronted, he responded that no one had told him he would have to give up his work or his friends. After all, there were Christian football players, Christian cowboys, Christian politicians; why not a Christian gangster?

It was only then that he was told about repentance. And at that point he wanted nothing to do with Christianity.

What happened to Mickey Cohen is an unhappy but unfortunately not so uncommon illustration of what happens when in our zeal to win people to Christ, we try to make the gospel more "appealing."

Repentance is one of the hard demands we often ignore. Contemporary sermons and books on the subject are rare. Because it can be an offense, as I discovered the morning I confronted twenty-five affluent business leaders with the need to repent, Christians often don't want to talk about it.

Jesus' evangelistic message, on the other hand, was plain and pointed: "Repent and believe in the gospel" (Mark 1:15). Like John the Baptist before him, Jesus consistently preached repentance. It is, in fact, the keynote of His message, the cornerstone upon which faith must rest.

To many, repentance conjures up images of breast beating, self-flagellation, or a monastic life of self-denial in sackcloth and ashes. The biblical meaning, however, is far less theatrical. Paul describes it as "sorrow over sin." "I now rejoice," he wrote to the Corinthians, "that you were made sorrowful to the point of repentance ... the sorrow that is according to the will of God produces repentance without regret, leading to salvation but the sorrow of the world produces death."

Repentance is, as one inmate in South Carolina said, "when you are so sorry that it hurts." When we truly understand the condition in us that causes us to lie, cheat and hate, we are inescapably made sorrowful. And that sorrow leads to a desire to change, to want the righteousness of God in place of our own sinful selves.

The Greek word for repentance found in the New Testament is *metanoia: meta,* meaning change, and *noia,* meaning mind. Repentance, as Christ preached it, is a changing of the mind, the intellect, the values. That inevitably produces a profound change of the heart and emotions, a total radical transformation from seeking to please self to seeking to please God. Repentance leads to nothing less than a human revolution.

The majority in prison with whom we work understand repentance; they can identify with the poignant moments of

Jesus' death on the cross, with two thieves hanging on either side. The first thief saw Jesus as a way out. "Are You not the Christ? Save Yourself and us!" he taunted. It's the way all of us instinctively react in tight spots. We call upon God to save our skins.

But the second thief understood the deeper spiritual reality. "We are receiving what we deserve for our deeds," he rebuked the first. "But this man has done nothing wrong." *That is repentance* — seeing one's sin and recognizing the holiness of God.

"Remember me," he then asked Jesus. And our Lord replied, "Truly, I say to you, today you will be with Me in paradise." *That is the result of repentance.*

Repentance is demanded not only for our individual sins, but for the sins for which we inescapably share responsibility as well. We are part and parcel of the society in which we live and the church we belong to. One of my favorite Old Testment figures is Nehemiah. He clearly understood the need to repent for himself and for the sins of his people. Before undertaking the seemingly impossible task of bringing the exiled Jews back to Jerusalem and rebuilding its walls, Nehemiah confessed "the sins of the sons of Israel which we have sinned against thee; I and my father's house have sinned." A repentant Nehemiah was greatly used by God; revival followed in the land.

The issue today is whether we are to be a church of Mickey Cohens or a church of Nehemiahs. Just as there is no individual salvation without repentance, so there can be no spiritual power in an unrepentant church. Southern Baptist scholar Foy Valentine sums it up in his magnificent new book *What Do You Do After You Say Amen?* "Without a fundamental change of mind about all sin, a stuttering, stumbling, stalling church can never act redemptively in a sinful world."

And the church acting redemptively in a fallen, sick world is the only key to survival and the hope of mankind.

July 1981

Chapter Thirty-eight

Can Revival Save America?
Part III

Ours is an age of paradoxes. In recent decades the world has discovered hitherto unimagined abundance, yet 12,000 people starve daily. More police are employed and prisons built than in any time in history, yet the crime rate accelerates at an alarming rate. This goes on and on.

But the greatest paradox of our time, I believe, is in the spiritual condition of America.

Recently pollster George Gallup reported that one in three American adults is born again, 84 percent believe the Ten Commandments are valid today, church attendance and missions giving are at record levels. Yet, despite these signs of religious resurgence, pornography is rampant, more children are aborted than born, violent crime is epidemic, and the family is disintegrating.

Historically, the most convincing evidence of spiritual awakenings have been their impact on society; a revived church inevitably changes the morality and values of a culture. Why is it not happening today?

One reason is our failure to heed the biblical call to repentance. Lack of repentance, I believe, is a root cause of church impotence in this materialistic, self-indulgent world.

Why is repentance so important? It is, as Dietrich Bonhoeffer wrote, "ultimate honesty," acknowledgement of what we are. A repentant heart produces tolerance and compassion for all other sinners, slaying the dragons of pride and self-righteousness.

Two of the most vivid examples of this I know are found on our PF staff. Two directors, both full-time and unpaid, are former business executives; one was president of one of America's largest insurance companies. Many people are amazed that these men seem more at home working with inmates than with their former business colleagues; but it should not really be so surprising: they have repentant hearts, which produce a genuine compassion for *all other* sinners.

Repentance, this true turning away from self, produces total dependance on God, which leads to reliance on prayer. Indeed, the significant Christian awakenings of past centuries have been marked by intense, fervent prayer.

I was reminded of the centrality of prayer to spiritual vitality when, during my recent trip to the Orient, I preached at the Full Gospel Church of Seoul, Korea, reportedly the largest church in the world. When I stood in the pulpit I was awed not by size — 15,000 people crammed in the sanctuary and 10,000 in overflow halls for just one of the six Sunday services—but by the sense of God's Spirit moving powerfully.

Later, as the pastor explained the workings of the church, the source of that power became clear. The church membership is divided into thousands of cell groups which meet every morning for two hours of Bible study and prayer. The real church is in the homes; Sunday morning is simply the culmination of a week of intense worship.

Prayer and Bible study are fruits of repentance; the life-blood of true spiritual movements.

One of my former White House colleagues was recently converted after a lifetime of pew sitting. At age fifty-one he is closing his lucrative law practice and will spend the next year in Bible college. The world might think him foolish, but he realizes that the truly repentant Christian hungers for knowledge of God and gratefully submits to the authority of Scripture and Christian doctrine.

Paul wrote, "I die daily," meaning that repentance is more than a one-time confession. Only as we continue our desire to change—the very essence of repentance—can we grow in grace and a continuing, deepening appreciation of God's grace and mercy which holds the key, I believe, to Christian impact on society, the answer to the great paradox of our time.

I've talked with hundreds of Prison Fellowship volunteers, often trying to determine why they selflessly toil in prisons. There is no glory, no fame for them there. Though their words may vary, their answer is always essentially the same. They see their service as the only possible response to God's grace. For it is out of gratitude to God for His grace and mercy that the Christian is moved to serve Christ in this sick world.

We share the Good News, feed the hungry, visit the imprisoned, seek justice for the oppressed and care for the widows and orphans, not because we are do-gooders or taken in by a social gospel, but out of appreciation for what God has done in our lives. When Christians by the millions practice this kind of obedience in all walks of life, we will see the culture profoundly impacted; for the strongholds of Satan cannot stand against that kind of holy power.

Only God can bring revival. But if we have any expectation or hope that He will so favor us, we'd best get down to serious and sacred business. And the place to begin, as Jesus commanded, is with repentant hearts.

August 1981

Chapter Thirty-nine

A Tale of Two Cities

It was an early evening before Thanksgiving when folks began arriving at the Georgia Avenue Church. A generation ago this red brick Victorian building towered majestically into the sky like the grand dame watching over this bustling neighborhood of old Atlanta.

But today the church is as desolate as the littered streets that surround it. Once-scrubbed white bungalows that line the blocks are soot-gray, crushed Coke cans lie in the gutters, sidewalks are cracked and overgrown.

But something exciting was in the air on this late November Saturday. Community residents were surprised to see cars begin to line the streets around the church, as friends of Prison Fellowship arrived from the four corners of Atlanta — not many outsiders defy the statistics in this crime-ridden area anymore.

Soon the sanctuary was full, the pews packed with black and white, rich, poor, and very poor. There were many ex-offenders, including a half dozen PF alumni: all God's people joyously together.

It was a farewell celebration as the community sent six convicts back to prison. The men had just spent two weeks painting, patching and insulating the homes of two neighborhood widows. And seated right next to them in the front pew were the two widows: one, eighty-three years old and blind from birth, the other, accompanied by her thirty-five-year-old retarded son.

As the service started, the Spirit's presence began to warm and illuminate the dark, musty sanctuary. The inmates had to choke back tears when they explained what the two-week experience had meant. So did the families in whose homes they had stayed. So did the rest of us.

No one could escape the powerful emotions of those magnificent moments. We tood together on a spiritual mountaintop, for we were seeing firsthand the church doing what it is supposed to do: caring for others out of obedience to Christ, proclaiming the Good News, and living it out with wholehearted joy.

Filled with that joy, I boarded my flight home and glanced at an evening paper. The headlines jolted me: the President and the Congress were deadlocked in an historic confrontation. After nine months of haggling and logrolling — and already two months into the government's new fiscal year — the Federal budget was still not approved. As tensions mounted and time ticked on, Congress proposed a temporary resolution to keep the government running through Thanksgiving.

But the resolution was $2 billion too much, the President said. And he threatened a veto that would result in the unprecedented closing down of the U.S. government the following Monday morning.

The picture was one of utter disarray. Neither side would budge, and no one seemed to want to avert a constitutional collision. The President's Budget Director, only months earlier heralded as the savior of the economy, was now on the sidelines, having embarrassed himself and the Administration by indiscreet comments to a reporter.

There was anger as well. The White House accused Congress of dragging its feet; Speaker of the House O'Neill said the President knew less about budgets than any President in his lifetime. Deafening volleys of charges and counter-charges exploded all weekend.

The President stood his ground, and on Monday, for the first time in history, the government shut down. That night, a weary, frustrated Congress passed a bill to Reagan's liking and mercifully went home — but only to fight the same battle again in mid-December.

As I settled into my seat, my thoughts alternated between the deeply moving service I'd just attended and the mortal combat going on at the same time in Washington.

I was struck by the contrast: on one hand a project of unity and reconciliation, on the other a bitter spirit of deep-seated divisiveness. Though weatherizing two homes is a far cry from putting together a $500 billion budget, both are attempts to meet human need. And how we go about that task tells us much about ourselves.

Washington is obsessed with plans and paperwork. Commenting on the budget debacle, Senator Mark Hatfield, chairman of the Appropriations Committee, put it well: "We got all of our computers running, and we had all of our calculations, all of our numbers, but we lost sight of people and programs."

But in Atlanta, people were concerned with people.

In Washington, the most powerful nation on earth seemed almost paralyzed; in Atlanta some folks saw a need, quickly got busy, and met it.

It was ugly and rancorous in Washington, while the love in Atlanta was overpowering.

The contrast is instructive; it yields important insight into our troubled times.

Government in a democracy is but a mirror reflection of the people; consequently, the budget impasse is but a symptom of a deeper malaise. One wonders whether egocentricity and materialism have so infiltrated the American value structure as to sap our nation of its capacity to act, to rise above partisan or selfish interests. The willingness to pull together for the common good is, after all, the cement which holds the loose bricks of democracy together.

That willingness, in the final analysis, is a question of human spirit and purpose; indeed a moral question. So, too, the answer to the dilemma of these times is a moral answer. Our renewed sense of responsibility — of caring about one another — will come not from power-seeking politicians, but from the hearts of compassionate individuals. And Christians must set clear examples of that caring.

That's why projects like Atlanta are so meaningful. Eleven churches, four organizations, and a host of committed individuals put aside differences between them to work together for a common need.

We undertook the winterization program to demonstrate that nonviolent inmates could be more effectively employed working in community projects, rather than vegetating in overcrowded, costly jail cells. And on that score, it was a great success: these men were doing work which was redemptive for them, beneficial to society, and cost the taxpayers nothing.

But I think the project's significance goes far beyond proving out an effective alternative to incarceration. It shows also an alternative to disunity and paralysis. What happened in Atlanta — people caring for others out of obedience to Christ — if repeated across America, can speak powerfully to a country nearly consumed with selfish greed. And that is the prophetic witness our nation so urgently needs.

January 1982

Chapter Forty

Religion and Politics:
The Hidden Peril

As I write this two weeks remain in the 1984 campaign. But whatever its outcome, one election result is already clear: the way in which the red-hot issue of religion and politics was debated poses grave concerns for the future of the church in America.

According to most polls, the public resented the issue. That's not surprising, I suppose, considering the daily scare headlines. Some hand-wringing alarmists warned of "religious ayatollahs," and even a "state-established religion."

What nonsense! Does any serious observer really suppose that a government-imposed religious establishment will arise, phoenix-like, from the fractured manifestation of religion in the U.S. today?

Consider that within Protestantism, new denominations appear and disappear like pop stars and space movies. The Roman Catholic Church, once a well-ordered ship, has, since Vatican II, tossed upon turbulent seas of division. Evangelicals are debating what was once a cardinal doctrine — the inerrancy of Scripture; and fundamentalists, for all their newfound political punch, refuse any common creed.

Consider also the majority in our culture who are indifferent to religion, and the minority who are passionately opposed to it, and one is hard pressed to understand the hysteria.

A second alarmist scare tactic has been to charge that the "wall of separation" between church and state was, like the wall of Jericho, in danger of being blown down — not by Joshua's trumpet, but by Jerry Falwell's.

More nonsense! That wall was erected to protect the church from the domination of government, not vice versa. And Christians were in the forefront of the unique American experiment known as separation of church and state. For they believed, as we do today, that since the state could not transform the human soul — only the Spirit of God could do that — government should neither attempt to establish nor interfere with the church. But to suggest that the purpose of the church and state separation was to keep religion out of politics betrays abysmal ignorance of our history.

For believers and non-Christians alike understood that public policies had to emerge from a moral consensus. For 200 years Christians have actively pursued biblical justice and righteousness in society; consider the abolitionist movement and the establishment of public education, public hospitals, prison reform, and in the twentieth century, prohibition and civil rights, to mention but a few examples.

Religiously founded values have been the cutting edge in shaping our national character. And through all this — until the recent campaign — no one has feared that the Christian religion was being "established" or that such morality was being "imposed" upon an unwilling people.

But the furor over these counterfeit issues has obscured the real problem: the way in which the opposing political camps have, for partisan advantage, polarized attitudes toward religion's role in society.

One side has made impassioned appeals for faith in God and country; though well intentioned, this civil religion uses God as a prop for the state. One recent President summed it up when he said that American government makes no sense "unless it is founded in a deeply felt religious faith — *and I don't care what it is*." This "faith in faith" reduces Christianity to a generic religion, and God to a vague deity who wears an American flag in His lapel.

The other side has argued that "in America our faith has always been intensely personal," confining religion to the church and home. New York Governor Cuomo's much-publicized speech at Notre Dame argued that an office-holder who professes to be a sincere Christian can advocate positions clearly contrary to the church's teaching.

So God's truth is only binding if approved by majority vote? This kind of logic gives sophistry a bad name. It also makes a mockery of the Christian faith. Yet commentators fell over backwards lauding the governor's speech.

Now the tragedy is that in the campaign's aftermath, many, including Christians, will fall into the trap of believing that religion's proper role is one or the other of these politically-defined alternatives.

But both positions deny the Lordship of Christ, and thus are dangerous counterfeits. For biblical Christianity declares that civil or generic religion is idolatry, and privatized faith is no faith at all.

And biblical Christianity also demands that the church never allow the gospel to be made hostage to any political agenda, but rather that as Christians, we be free to advocate whatever political position best reflects biblical truth.

Thus our challenge is clear: we must reject the false religions raised in the '84 campaign, and reassert the ageless truth that Christ is Lord, King of kings.

That birthright is much too precious to be traded for a mess of political pottage.

November 1984

Chapter Forty-one

Christ or Culture?
Lessons From Abroad

Two meetings — Billy Graham's conference on evangelism in Amsterdam and Prison Fellowship International's first symposium in Belfast — proved exhilarating experiences. Yet they were also deeply disturbing, upsetting a lot of comfortable notions about what it means to be a Christian in today's world.

First, Amsterdam. What a magnificent sight: 5,000 evangelists packed into a huge auditorium, faces radiating excitement. Though they were of every color and language, there seemed an immediate unity. No one could fail to be moved by the spirit and commitment of those attending this historic meeting. In fact, I can't get some of them out of my mind.

Like George Chan, a Chinese brother imprisoned eighteen years for his faith; or the couple, also Chinese, who refused to renounce Christ. Forced to watch while their eighteen-year-old son's heart was cut out, they were then dragged off to prison — and could communicate only by singing hymns across the walls separating male and female inmates. I was also struck by the sacrificial commitment of hundreds who arrived in Amsterdam with everything they owned wrapped in bedrolls or paper sacks.

During my speech one evening, I described prisons as "hell-holes." It's a term I've used thousands of times, but this night it provoked an unprecedented reaction. A murmur swept the auditorium, growing in intensity as interpreters translated, followed by a ripple of amens, then applause.

At first I was startled; only later, when I talked with delegates, did I understand. Many Third-World evangelists have been in prison; many more know what it means to be oppressed, persecuted. Without realizing it, when I talked about suffering and prisons, I struck a sensitive chord. Cultural barriers came down — fast.

Following Amsterdam, more than 145 delegates from thirty-four countries gathered in Belfast for PFI's symposium — a remarkable turnout for this first meeting ever of Christians working in prisons around the world. Again I was struck by the commitment and intensity of those who came. On the edges of their chairs, notebooks out, delegates were straining to pack in as much as they could, to study, to learn, to share the fellowship of our common calling.

They were a remarkable group. People like Aradom Tedla, former director general of Ethiopia's Ministry of Law and Justice, jailed after the Communist takeover. Miraculously released, he left Ethiopia and now works for prisoners' rights — as does Roger Arienda, a former Marxist, converted in prison, where he led thousands of fellow prisoners to Christ.

Their stories were representative of so many others — tales of persecution, of deprivation, of witnessing at risk in hostile cultures.

I've heard marvelous testimonies before, I thought, *but why are these so different? Just like the conferees in Amsterdam. Why is their faith so vibrant, so alive?*

The question nagged me for days — until I heard the testimony of a furloughed prisoner. Converted after coming within hours of death on an IRA hunger strike, Liam put the issue plainly: "I realized I had to choose — between the Republican movement [IRA] and Christ."

Liam chose to follow Christ. That choice meant perhaps not just the scorn of his former compatriots, but the loss of friends, family, maybe even death, for those who leave the IRA often face serious repercussions.

Liam's simple words made me understand what should be an obvious truth. To live as a Christian in most of the world involves a clear, often painful choice: it means choosing Christ over comfort, Christ over safety, Christ over material things, even Christ over family. It often means breaking radically with the status quo.

It is difficult for those of us in the West to understand this. For in our "Christian" culture it's the expected thing to be found in church on Sundays. And it's comfortable to be Christian. In fact, some pastors teach that if we merely ask, our generous Father will shower us with all the "blessings" our affluent society has to offer.

Being Christian in the West seems to mean joining the power structure, but in much of the rest of the world it means standing against it, risking everything. Our Third-World brethren in particular understand the hard truth that the structures of this world are fallen — and the gospel, therefore, is counterculture.

Curiously, I found myself almost envious of my brothers who had lost everything for the gospel's sake; for in the process they had found what I, in many ways, was still seeking.

Of course, the danger in making such sweeping comparisons is that we create guilt trips for ourselves and others, or unfairly denigrate our churches. After all, American Christians provide the bulk of missions support for worldwide evangelization; and across the U.S. are pockets of serious Christians seeking a deeper communion with God.

But the fervent believers I met in Belfast and Amsterdam reminded me that the Christian life demands a hard choice, one that we must make no less than our brothers and sisters in less fortunate areas. Our choice must be the same — Christ over comfort, over security, over success. Christ over all.

No, I haven't been able to get these brothers and sisters abroad out of my mind. I hope and pray that I won't.

September 1983

Chapter Forty-two

Beware of "Politics as Usual"

During the great New York City blackout of 1977, a young boy became inordinately fearful. Under the anxious questioning of his parents, he confessed: at the very moment the lights went out, he had kicked a power-line pole. As darkness descended over the entire city, the boy concluded he had caused the catastrophe, and was panic-stricken he would be punished.

I thought of this story recently when Attorney General William French Smith announced that the crime rate was going down — and, he triumphantly told reporters, his administration's policies were responsible.

I can't really blame the Attorney General for making political hay out of good statistics. I did the same thing regularly when I was in the White House.

This kind of political posturing is predictable, particularly in the months before a national election. One enlightened prison official, New York Commissioner Thomas Couglin, foresaw the downward trend in crime months ago, and said, with refreshing candor, "everybody's going to take credit for it."

But for the Attorney General, or any politician, to take credit is, I'm afraid, a little bit like the boy in New York: if the lights go out when you kick the pole, you must be responsible.

Let's look at the facts: First, the federal government has very limited jurisdiction for law enforcement; 90 percent of all crimes are prosecuted by states and municipalities. Less than 7 percent of all inmates are in federal institutions.

Second, there is no evidence that "get tough" policies reduce crime. A few years ago an official in the National Institute of Corrections (an arm of Mr. Smith's own department) concluded after his own study that there is no correlation between the rate of imprisonment and the crime rate: that is, longer sentences *do not* result in less crime.

Recent comparisons bear this out. In 1983, Florida employed sentencing guidelines and release, reducing its prison population by 5.4 percent; Florida's crime rate decreased 6.9 percent. California, on the other hand, really "got tough," and increased its prison population by 13.6 percent; crime went down 6.7 percent, a little less than Florida.

No, the major factor in the crime drop is something for which no politician can claim credit. It is simply the changing age of the population, the end of the post-World War II baby boom.

In the late sixties and seventies, the baby boom created a surge of young people; many communities were nearly bankrupted with school bond issues. But now the baby boomers are in their thirties.

A recent *Businessweek* article observed, "A new fault line is cracking the foundation of American society. It is ripping through political parties, upsetting old voting patterns, undermining traditional corporate structures, and reshaping the marketplace."

These changing demographics affect crime as well. The vast majority of crimes are committed by people in their teens and twenties; statistics show that as people grow older, they become less likely to break the law. Since the number of people in the crime-prone age is now declining, so is the crime rate.

This evidence should make us wary of political posturing. Sure, politicians will take credit for any encouraging statistics — that's politics as usual. But we'd better not make policy based on silly campaign statements. For the simplistic mindset which would ignore the baby boom would inevitably advocate more prisons and longer sentences.

One official recently admitted to me, "If we don't get the prisons built now, the public will never go along with it in a few years when the baby boom passes and the population drops." He must have sensed my horror: he immediately added, "Well, of course, we need the new prisons anyway."

But we don't need more prisons. The prison population will rapidly decline as the number of Americans in the crime-prone age declines. In fact, it has already started to happen; the rate of increase in prison population dropped dramatically the first six months of this year.

And prisons don't rehabilitate anyway. This is why Prison Fellowship and our affiliate, Justice Fellowship, have advocated alternatives to incarceration for nonviolent offenders, instead of new prison construction.

So we have some good news and some bad news. The good is that crime appears to be dropping in America. The bad is that we may do some dumb and wasteful things if we believe that so-called "tough" criminal justice policies are the cause.

The fact is, we must not pour more tax dollars down the prison construction drain, or we will face in the prisons the same consequence of the baby boom that the public schools faced a decade ago — expensive, empty institutions whose occupants have all "graduated."

And that's a high price to pay for "politics as usual."

October 1984

Chapter Forty-three

The Political Illusion

During an evening newscast, I watched a parade of political candidates promise to end the arms race, eliminate the deficit, settle the Middle East, and produce full employment. It was breathtaking.

Then I tried to remember — and couldn't — a single instance in which a candidate for any office, from city councilman to President, had ever admitted any problem that he or she could not solve once elected.

But in truth many problems can't be cured — at least not the way the politicians promise. And even officials in the most powerful offices sometimes discover they're not so powerful after all.

I remember one Friday afternoon in 1970 when President Nixon called me into his office. "I want an executive order creating a commission to study aid to nonpublic schools," he snapped. "Have it on my desk by 9 A.M. Monday!" Mr. Nixon was frustrated that the creation of the commission, a campaign pledge, had been ignored by the Justice Department for eighteen months.

Simple enough, I thought. All I had to do was to find the

right form, check it out with other staffers, and have it typed. Then bedlam hit. John Erlichman protested that I was "invading his area." The Attorney General was on the phone, as was the Commissioner of Education. Memos began flying back and forth as the bureaucracy suddenly came alive.

The battle that began that weekend went on for months. Eventually the order was issued, only to be soon forgotten.

This was no isolated instance. Career bureaucrats outlast Presidents, and are experts at stymieing orders they don't like. Many programs are deadlocked between Congress and the President; some agencies, after being launched with great fanfare, simply watch the problems they were created to solve steadily worsen.

Yet politicians of both parties continue to promise — and the electorate continues to expect — political solutions to all our ills. We go through the same cycle every election year. Why?

Two decades ago, Jacques Ellul, the eminent French historian, answered the question in a remarkably prophetic book, *The Political Illusion*. Ellul theorized that modern man increasingly turns to the state for answers to his problems — even though the state cannot solve them. Politicians perpetuate the myth that it can since the illusion perpetuates their power; the media willingly collaborates since their coverage of government fuels their own power — and profits — as well.

The result, Ellul wrote, is a "boundless growth" of the state, with an insatiable appetite for power. (Of special interest to us in Prison Fellowship's ministry, Ellul argues that independent groups which involve people in meeting society's needs are the only way to lessen dependence upon government and its eventual totalitarian control.)

We Christians, of all people, should see through the political illusion. We should understand that the real problems of our society are, at their root, moral and spiritual. Institutions and politicians are limited in what they can do.

Certainly that is so in the criminal justice field. Crime is the result of wrong moral choices. Laws are needed to restrain evil, but penal institutions can't deal with the ultimate problem: the human heart. That's why the gospel of Christ is the only real answer.

Even in foreign policy, governments are not all-powerful, as we are accustomed to think. The Marine presence in Lebanon was no deterrent to the centuries-old civil strife there. The British have learned the same lesson in Ulster.

Or take the example of Poland. Against the "powerful" array of Soviet divisions, thousands of schoolchildren marched with their crucifixes held high, successfully resisting the Communist government's edict to remove crosses from their classrooms. Where is the real power in Poland? Certainly not in the Politburo.

The political illusion poses two grave dangers: first, as political solutions fail and problems worsen, people become cynical, and in time, alienated from their own political process. The second is that the political illusion fosters a false security: the government is promising to deal with our problems, so we don't have to bother. It lets us off the hook.

Many of the government's much-ballyhooed programs of the sixties (few of which ever got any money to the needy) offer a case in point. As social programs mushroomed, private agencies helping the poor declined. Because of the illusion that the government was taking care of things, individual people stopped actively caring for others.

So beware of the political illusion. Of course, government is ordained by God to maintain order, promote justice, and restrain sin. But listen with healthy skepticism to inflated political rhetoric. Political institutions provide no panaceas to the ills of our age, no matter how attractive they sound; and they are surely no substitute for individual responsibility.

I'd like to recommend that you read Ellul's book, *The Political Illusion*. But I can't. For in the most revealing commentary on our surrender to the illusion the book warns of, it is out of print. No market, the publisher says.

June 1984

Chapter Forty-four

Reflections on a Conversion

A few years ago our nation was gripped by the beginnings of the most explosive political scandal of the century. As Watergate unfolded, several men were in the thick of it, with the daily barrage of headlines painting me, Charles Colson, Nixon's Special Counsel and "hatchet man," the toughest of the lot. Then, as investigation stepped up and the news stories flowed, came headlines even more startling than the daily fare of missing tapes, secret deals and hush money: "Colson Turns to God." For weeks cartoonists feasted, politicians scoffed, the public smirked. My commitment to Jesus Christ became one of the most publicized conversions of the century.

A decade has passed since August 12, 1973, the day I committed my life to Christ. So it seems only natural to answer some of the questions posed recently by a friend. It is my hope that these candid reflections offer insights into the struggles I've undergone as well as testimony to God's great work in my life.

Did you have any idea what you were in for when you committed your life to Christ?

No way. For all I knew I was one of the first four or five people in the world who had ever done it. Seriously, I had never heard the world *evangelical*; the only Christian book I knew was *Mere Christianity*; Tom Phillips was the only person I'd ever met who said he'd accepted Christ. I had absolutely no idea my decision would mean prison, then ministry, that my whole view of life — in every area — would be turned completely upside down. I couldn't possibly have imagined what was ahead.

What were your first impressions of Christians?

Obviously, Harold Hughes' embracing me the first night we met when we had been political enemies was completely overwhelming. I had never imagined grown men saying they "loved" each other. When I was in the White House, Haldeman and I vied for the President's favor. And then we'd both quarrel with Erlichman or Kissinger; another aide would agree with me in private and then with the President back away to make himself look good at my expense; or I would turn around and do the same thing to him. We were all constantly competing for power. In the Christian world, while we have human competitiveness and disagreements within organizations, it's a totally different feeling because your own personal interests are less than the interest of the cause.

Why is that different from politics?

After coming out of forty years of secular life and then spending a dozen years in the Christian life, I can tell you: the relationships people have in Christ don't exist in the secular world. I could never go back. There's not enough money or power in the world to draw me back into the kind of partisan bickering that went on in politics — or in my law firm, for that matter. I just wouldn't want to live that way.

Critics say you were a power broker for Nixon, and now

you're a power broker for Jesus — that you've just transferred your loyalties.

If they're right, that's the best trade anyone's ever made. No, the question does worry me, because all my life I've been ambitious, hard-driving, a perfectionist desiring to win, very idealistic. So have I just transferred my loyalties? To be absolutely honest, I can't ever be certain what motivates me. Jeremiah tells us that nothing is more deceitful than the human heart — and he's right. I *think* I'm in this ministry because of my love for the Lord and desire to serve Him, but maybe it's because Chuck Colson has to be in the center of things and has to be the big organizer and doer. And I'm out of the political business, so I'm in the religous business.

How do you deal with those doubts?

I'll probably always have them, if I'm honest. I really don't know myself that well — nobody does. It's the same problem Luther wrote about. If you leave the monastery, you're going to be subjected to the temptations of the world, but if you don't you're not going to do much good for the Lord. So go out, Luther said: "Go and sin, and sin boldly." That quote has been taken out of context, of course, but it means we go out and live for Christ realizing the risks of doing so. And so I have to serve Christ in this ministry, realizing the risk that I may be deceiving myself as to why I do it.

How do you see yourself — that ambitious, hard-driving perfectionist — as having changed in the years since your conversion?

God doesn't give you a whole set of new gifts when He converts you. Paul the zealous persecutor became Paul the zealous propagator of the faith. We're all like that. God simply redirects our gifts and priorities. My priorities before were power, wealth, fame; today I believe they're knowing and loving God, my relationships with my family, which have become *much* more meaningful to me, and my desire to serve the Lord.

What effects do you see that service having?

Well, Prison Fellowship's growth and ministry have been amazing. God is raising a mighty movement, a fellowship that's penetrating the prisons. That's great news, of course; but at the same time I'm frustrated, preaching a message to the church, challenging Christians to make an impact for Christ in every walk of life, and seeing crowds respond enthusiastically — and yet every moral indicator shows we're going down the tubes. It's like shoveling sand against the waves. The only thing that redeems that is knowing God calls me to be faithful, not successful. The end result is in His hands, not mine. So I'll keep shoveling the sand.

Does that make you feel burned out?
Yes, sometimes. A real occupational hazard.

How do you deal with that?
The only way is to find time for reflective reading and study. For me, one of the most exciting things about life in Christ is that I feel like a kid going back to school — I really love to study, and the Bible is limitless. It constantly gives me a fresh perspective.

How do you feel about being a "Christian celebrity"?
It's terrifying. I've walked onto platforms literally churning inside, in fear that I would fail to be a worthy witness, or say something biblically incorrect. I can't think of anything worse. A New York bishop stood up before a gay pride demonstration

recently saying AIDS is not the judgment of God; that same day a Syrian ayatollah said he would promise a special reward in heaven for anyone who assassinated Arafat. I thought, here on two sides of the world are two of the most ridiculous statements I've ever heard. So incredibly presumptuous. Who is to say AIDS is or is not the judgment of God? Who can promise God has a special reward in heaven for particular assassins? The only way you can speak for God with certainty is to speak from the Bible. And the longer I'm a Christian, the more I'm in fear of misinterpreting the Bible. It's an awesome responsibility.

What have been your greatest struggles?

Well, the biggest struggle in lifestyle was to quit smoking. And the main thing I constantly have to deal with is pride. I understand why Paul said, "I die daily." Then there's the celebrity syndrome, the loss of privacy, being held up as something often I'm not, the responsibility that goes with being so public, realizing how many people will judge Christianity by what I do. That's intense pressure sometimes.

What do you think will happen in your life in the next few years?

I have no idea what the future holds; it's good we don't. If I had known what was ahead a few years ago, I would have fled in terror. But I do know one thing, *Jesus is who He says He is.* Knowing Him is all that matters. At the risk of sounding triumphal, I wouldn't trade the toughest day of the last few years — which includes those in prison — for the best day of the forty years before.

August 1983

Chapter Forty-five

Preaching *and* Caring

"Your job, Mr. Colson, is to bring the gospel to prisoners. What are you doing talking about reform?"

A young man asked me that question recently after I'd spoken on the need for changes in our criminal justice system. His inquiry is a fair one, and one I'm being asked more frequently. It deserves a reply:

First, as a citizen, one cannot help but question the billions being spent for a system which has such a tragic record of failure. When some studies show that four out of five crimes are committed by ex-offenders, one has to ask whether prisons are correctional institutions, or "graduate schools of crime" as they're sometimes called. Sadly, most people released from prison are going to get in trouble again, commit another crime and, at great cost to society, end up back behind bars. The prison isn't necessarily to blame, but shouldn't we as taxpayers be looking for better answers?

Then, too, I lived in prison for seven months. I've seen the waste in human, as well as in monetary, terms—and I've not been able to forget.

But what makes the issue particularly Christian? What business is it of ours to be concerned about prison conditions or the policies and practices of our criminal justice system?

A recent experience may provide at least part of the answer.

In October 1979, I visited one of the meanest prisons in America. On the day I arrived, 1,200 inmates were being released from an unusually long "lockdown." Following the murder of a guard, all inmates had been confined to their cells for twenty-three hours a day — for four months! Most officials and inmates expected violence. In fact, the official who met me at the gate said, "I hope you can do something. I don't know what, but do something — anything. This place is ready to explode." Trained riot police were in readiness.

Never have I been more aware of hatred and bitterness inside a prison. You could smell it in the air and see it on the faces of inmates. Many guards were openly fearful.

After touring the protective custody and segregation areas and the hospital, I was able to speak to about a hundred maximum security inmates gathered in the prison auditorium.

The next week we held a seminar in that prison. After the first day, nine inmate leaders asked to meet with our instructor. They told him that a riot had been planned for the week before — on the day I'd spoken, in fact. Five guards were to have been killed in revenge for the four-month lockdown, and for abuses of which the inmates believed they had been victims.

But, the inmate leaders explained, they had listened to my remarks; one of them who had been converted to Christ persuaded the other leaders to postpone the planned riot. "We think we can trust Colson and you," the leader said.

It was no joking matter. Like it or not, we were suddenly in the middle — on one side a chance for healing and peace; on the other side, the prospect of death and bloodshed.

At that point, no one stopped to ask whether prison conditions were our proper concern. We are ministers of the gospel message, to be sure; but to tell a group of angry inmates that we are interested only with preaching a spiritual message and not with their actual conditions — then literally a matter of life and death — would have been unthinkable.

Over the ensuing weeks, two of our staff held a series of meetings with inmate leaders and prison officials. An uneasy truce emerged, and Prison Fellowship became intermediary between the prison population and staff.

Through the nearly eighteen months that we've worked in that tense place, we've continuously presented the gospel without compromise. Our teaching is unashamedly Christian. Men are being converted to Christ; the Christian fellowship is growing and thriving; we helped start a fellowship among the guards.

But we have also been confronted with questions of justice and human dignity and we've *had* to care about them. And we have. I visited most of the political leaders of the state, many of whom are deeply concerned. Important legislation has been drafted. A committee of Prison Fellowship friends has been organized to help. Prison officials are cooperative and the courts have recently handed down some encouraging rulings. And so, help is on the way for one of the most dangerous prison situations I've encountered anywhere.

As I've reflected on the experience, I've realized that it simply is not possible to minister in prison without being concerned for inmates' welfare, and for basic principles of God's justice for all men — "the just and the unjust" alike. This is called common grace.

It's also common sense. No pastor would preach to a congregation about spiritual needs if, for example, they were suddenly homeless from some natural disaster. In fact, in between sermons, he'll probably be out helping his parishioners rebuild their homes.

The fact is, then, there's no way to tell people about Jesus without exhibiting towards them the same love and concern that He did during His earthly ministry. Surely, there is no dicholomy in Scripture between *preaching* the Good News and *caring* about human dignity and human needs.

Nor can one read the Old Testament without being gripped by our God's passion for justice. He cares deeply about how people live, and especially those who are the oppressed and forgotten. He tell us to care, too: "Learn to do good, seek justice, reprove the ruthless, defend the orphan, plead for the widow" (Isaiah 1:17).

Some changes in our prison and justice system are desperately and urgently needed. Precisely because we serve the One who brings forth "justice and righteousness," we must act.

January 1981

Chapter Forty-six

Called to Faithfulness

It's a dangerous and misguided policy to measure God's blessing by standards of visible, tangible, material "success."

The reason is simply that often the evidence of God's blessing will not be discernible to us. Many ministries and men of faith down the centuries have passed through great periods of trial, and even deprivation, when there was no sign whatever that God was pleased with them or their work. And yet in retrospect, it is clear that He was — although often in ways which were unknown and unexpected at the time. As the Book of Job emphasizes time and again, God's blessing may come despite of — or even because of — what the world regards as "failure." The crucifixion of our Lord Jesus is the most astonishing of all examples of this crucial truth, for precisely when the world and its powers of darkness thought that God and man alike had utterly failed, He was establishing His kingdom with power and grace.

Too much today, we evangelicals attempt to gauge the "success" of our work in terms of church membership, new construction, new programs, national publicity or prestige, or souls saved per pew. The inference is that when things are prospering "God is blessing us" and, conversely, that when things are going poorly, or unpublicized, God's blessing is not upon the work or it is unimportant.

This tendency of holding up success as proof of God's blessing is one of the most heretical notions abroad in American Christendom today.

Quite obviously, by exploiting the technological wonders of the age, almost anyone can "succeed" if by success is meant national exposure via the media — or even thousands of supporters and their dollars. A recent news account, for example, told of a "ministry" that had raised millions of dollars, even though it had failed to do any of the things its promotional materials promised.

The ministry consisted only of a famous person and a huge bank account. But does that money and notriety necessarily mean that God has "blessed" that work? Or has the so-called ministry merely been able to manipulate the mass media to raise dollars for no actual — but only an advertised — purpose?

The answer, of course, is obvious.

This is a key reason we at Prison Fellowship are careful about the statistics we use about our own work. Certainly we believe God's hand is upon us and, yes, that He is blessing us. But not because of the statistics — encouraging though they sometimes are.

Rather, we believe it as a matter of faith, and because of His promises, and we must continuously use the measure of our obedience to the guidelines of His Word as the real — and only — standard of our "success," not some more supposedly tangible or glamorous scale.

For in the last and best analysis, the real test of any ministry's success is not the number of its converts, or the size of its budget, or its reputation, or even the fruits of its labors —

significant though they might appear to be. Jesus warns us in Matthew 7:23, 24 not to bank on self-evaluation, because it's possible to be doing seemingly "good works" only to be completely off the mark of His will.

That mark isn't "success," it's faithfulness. God calls us, not to success, but to faith—obedience and trust and service—and He bids us to be unconcerned with measuring the merits of our work the way the world does. We are to sow; He will reap as He pleases.

"Whatever you do, do all to the glory of God," the Apostle Paul exhorted the early church.

Let that—and nothing else—be the standard of our Christian "success."

October 1980

Index